"An extraordinary account of one of Vermont's most ~~~~ ~~~~ ~~~~~, *Winters' Time*, with its twists and turns, internecine convolutions, and high political drama, is revealed in perfect measure by the best of possible narrators. Vermont jurist Jeffrey Amestoy balances the arcane, the historical, and the dramatic aspects of this case with a lawyer's attention to detail and a novelist's compelling touch. An excellent read and highly recommended."

—Archer Mayor, author of the Joe Gunther mysteries.

"Jeffrey Amestoy reconstructs a forgotten story in American history— one that reveals tensions of class, gender, and family, and gives the reader a glimpse of justice in the 1920s. *Winters' Time* combines legal history, true crime, a cast of Vermont characters, and America's famous 'attorney for the damned.' And it's all told beautifully, with careful scholarship, and at a pace that keeps the book in your hands."

—Randall Tietjen, editor of *In the Clutches of the Law:
Clarence Darrow's Letters* (2013).

"Former Chief Justice Jeffrey Amestoy is the perfect scholar to write this story of the time Clarence Darrow appeared before the Vermont Supreme Court on behalf of a defendant accused of murder. That court had to work hard to ignore the reputation of America's greatest advocate. Amestoy's insight into the legal and social issues of the *Winters* case is grounded in his own experience on the court, and his understanding of the special pressures felt by his predecessor John H. Watson is particularly intriguing."

—Paul S. Gillies, author of *The Law of the Hills:
A Judicial History of Vermont* (2019).

Winters' Time

Winters' Time

A Secret Pledge, a Severed Head, and the Murder that Brought America's Most Famous Lawyer to Vermont

Jeffrey L. Amestoy

Vermont Historical Society

BARRE AND MONTPELIER

Library of Congress Cataloging-in-Publication Data
available upon request.

Printed in the United States of America
27 26 25   1 2 3

Text design by James F. Brisson
Cover design by Andrew Liptak

ISBN: 978-0-934720-84-7 (paperback)
978-0-934720-85-4 (epub)
978-0-934720-86-1 (ePDF)

First Printing, September 2025

FOR FRED REMINGTON

CONTENTS

CONTENTS

ACKNOWLEDGMENTS

A HALF-CENTURY AGO a new attorney sat in the "lawyers' room" of the superior court in Woodstock, Vermont, awaiting his first courtroom appearance. To mask his anxiety, he pointed to a photograph on the wall and asked a senior lawyer—they were *all* senior to him—about the picture. "The most sensational murder trial in Vermont's history," one replied.

I was that new lawyer, and as I look back on a time both impossibly long ago to young readers, and only yesterday to older ones, I remember thinking, "that might make a good book." Whether I have written one is for readers to decide. So too, is whether the detour I took made it a better story. But I do know that whatever merit *Winters' Time* may have owes much to many.

I thank the Vermont Historical Society, its board, and its director, Steve Perkins, for their faith in the project and the author. My only regret in working with VHS is that I realize how much I have missed by not becoming an active member earlier in my life. I encourage readers of this book who are not members to look at the extraordinary array of VHS offerings. There are stories from your own community's history that are as interesting as this one, written by local authors who have a better right to be called historians than do I.

It was a delight—a word seldom used in this context—to work with editor Alan Berolzheimer. Alan immediately perceived how the Winters case is a lens through which readers could view justice, gender, class, and celebrity in the Roaring Twenties of rural Vermont. He let me know when I smudged the lens (it was usually when my fingers had too much law on them). Any smudges that remain are mine alone.

My research drew on many sources but two works were essential. *The Law of the Hills* by Paul Gillies was indispensable to me and will always be to any student of Vermont legal history. "Indispensable" is the right term too for Paul, a lawyer-historian without peer. *In the Clutches of the Law: Clarence Darrow's Letters*, edited by Randall Tietjen (also a lawyer), includes letters critical to my story. Without the benefit of his exhaustive and scholarly work it would have taken months of archival research for me to find them—and I may not have.

Archival research can be rewarding if one is fortunate enough to work in excellent archives with excellent archivists. The Vermont State Archives and Records Administration (VSARA) has both. I am particularly indebted to Mariessa Dobrick and her staff for their responsiveness to my many requests. Mariessa has taken on new challenges elsewhere, but Angela Valentinetti, Kara Koenig, and Andrew Rais were equally responsive to questions that multiplied the nearer I got to deadline. Thanks too, to Gail Wiese at the Vermont Historical Society's Leahy Library, where the beauty of the reference room brightens even the darkest of Vermont days.

Invariably, an author's journey from idea to book is marked by surprises—welcome and unwelcome. When I made my first inquiry to the Windsor Historical Society about the Winters case I was surprised to learn that a distant relative of Cecelia Gullivan's had just been there to begin her own research. "I can ask if she wishes to talk to you," said Kathryn Grover, the estimable WHS director.

Christine Simonson was a welcome surprise. Cecelia Gullivan was a first cousin of Chris's maternal grandmother and had been her grandmother's bridesmaid. A small box left by her grandmother contained a newspaper clipping of the terrible murder. Chris and her cousin, Jane Looney, began their own search. They were intrepid investigators, generously sharing the results of their findings.

Kathryn Grover's invaluable assistance extended beyond her role of putting me in touch with Cecelia Gullivan's relatives. Her responses to my requests were always timely despite other demands. Windsor can claim to be the site of as much significant Vermont history as any town in the state. It is well served by its historical society and Kathryn.

I am grateful for help in locating photographs used in *Winters' Time*. Christine Simonson graciously provided the striking picture of Cecelia Gullivan. John Alexander of the American Precision Museum went above and beyond in responding to my request for assistance in dating a photograph of workers at the Cone Automatic plant. Thanks as well to Teri Corsones and Alison Johannensen of the Vermont judiciary; Theo Advent of the Springfield Art and Historical Society; the Hartford Historical Society; and the Windsor Station Restaurant.

ACKNOWLEDGMENTS

David Tartter, appellate lawyer and legal researcher par excellence, expressed astonishment equal to mine upon learning that the severed head of a victim was admitted into evidence without objection. I asked him to determine if there was another such case in the country. He could not find one and those of us who have had the privilege of working with David know that if he could not find a precedent, it probably does not exist.

Family members volunteered—or were drafted—to assist the author. Nancy and Christina Amestoy were of immense help from beginning to end. Nancy provided perceptive insight when I looked for guidance in shaping the narrative. Without Christina's assistance in preparing the manuscript and endnotes, this would still be a work in progress. Susan Amestoy was a patient and thoughtful audience even when I referred to Darrow as Dana (the subject of my first book). I have promised not to write a book about Darwin.

Fred Remington, to whom this book is dedicated, is a boyhood friend from Rutland. Fred and I grew up in similar circumstances. They were not nearly as dire as those of John Winters. But neither the decades nor the neighborhoods that separate Winters' Rutland from ours make it unrecognizable. Close enough, at least, to know that one difference between our boyhood and his was kindness.

Winters' Time

PROLOGUE
The Letter

ON A MAY EVENING IN 1927, America's most famous lawyer, Clarence Darrow, surveyed a packed Dartmouth College auditorium. The title of his lecture, "Why I Oppose Capital Punishment," was controversial. Few Americans, none with the celebrity of Darrow, favored abolition of the death penalty. For the past decade, legislatures had raced to reintroduce capital punishment where it had been abolished. States experimented with new methods of execution.

Thirty miles from Hanover, New Hampshire, in neighboring Vermont, Windsor State Prison installed an electric chair to replace the gallows. Many Vermonters were awaiting the execution of John Winters, who was in the prison's "death cell." Three months earlier in a sensational trial that captured national attention, a jury had found him guilty of murdering a prominent Vermont businesswoman.

Clarence Darrow's fame—as great in the celebrity-crazed Roaring Twenties as that of Charles Lindbergh or Charlie Chaplin—owed much to the public's fascination with Darrow's uncanny ability to save murderers from execution. Three years before, in a case that transfixed the nation, Darrow saved from death the wealthy precocious teenagers Leopold and Loeb, who kidnapped and murdered fourteen-year-old Bobby Franks in a thrill killing. "I did it because I wanted to," said eighteen-year-old "Dickie" Loeb.[1]

For seventy-year-old Darrow, the Dartmouth lecture enabled him to emphasize the one principle—some said the only one—he consistently followed as a lawyer. "He had an 'insane desire' to save life," said a colleague summarizing Darrow's half-century as "attorney for the damned."[2]

But for Clarence Darrow, the Dartmouth talk was far removed from the urgency of life-and-death representation. "Darrow Plans to Retire" headlined the *New York Times* a month before. He was a grandfather and if he was now to give lectures instead of trying cases, Dartmouth—his only son, Paul, was a 1904 graduate—seemed a pleasant place to start.

When Darrow finished his remarks, he was surrounded by students as eager as any audience to be near fame. "One of the boys came to me and told me a lady wanted to see me and told me what it was all about. I told the boy he was crazy that no such thing could have happened," wrote Darrow to Paul, the next day.

"But I told him to bring her," continued Darrow, "and she showed me your letter. She said you were in no way to blame . . . She said she could raise a little money, and I told her I didn't want any. Of course, I will do all I can for her . . . I am sorry this has bothered you all these years."[3]

The 1904 letter the woman showed Clarence Darrow contained a promise: if ever she or her family needed help, Paul Darrow assured her that his father would assist her. Now, twenty-three years later, she was asking America's most renowned lawyer to make good on his own son's pledge.

"I need your help," Mrs. Arthur Cooley told Darrow. "My nephew John Winters is on Death Row in Vermont."[4]

⇒ 1 ⇐

The Accident

THE DARTMOUTH COLLEGE that welcomed Paul Darrow as a freshman in 1900 was not the Dartmouth of 1927 when his father spoke there. Three-quarters of the 800 male students were from Massachusetts, New Hampshire, and Vermont. Tuition was $100. There was no "Ivy League."

When Dartmouth's president sought to extend his college's reach, Harvard's president asked why he thought there could be any suitable students beyond New England. But Paul Darrow found fellow Chicagoans at Dartmouth. The college catalog noted that the Central Vermont Railway connected White River Junction, Vermont, to "points west (Chicago 30 hours)."

Adventurous arriving students could try novel "horseless carriages" for the short trip to the Hanover, New Hampshire, campus from White River Junction, where fifty passenger trains a day steamed through the station. Steam from trains and automobiles often spooked horses and "runaway horses posed a threat to pedestrians."[1]

In 1903, Paul's Dartmouth made a statement that Harvard could not ignore—Dartmouth's football team upset Harvard in the inaugural game at Harvard's Soldiers Field Stadium. If Paul participated in the celebration there's no record he did so excessively. Nor did he distinguish himself academically. He was by all accounts a sober young man.

On June 22, 1904, Paul Darrow was three days from his Dartmouth commencement. That day, Paul's classmate and president of the senior class, Peter Maguire, began a daily jaunt from campus across the Connecticut River bridge to Norwich, Vermont. Maguire took the walk so often that he made friends with five-year-old Harry Cooley, whose house was on a hill above the Norwich train depot.

Maguire would sometimes lift the little boy to a railing so he could see the arrival of trains at the Norwich station below. That sunny afternoon, Harry was already at the railing with a young friend. Maguire waved to

3

both and continued on his way. As the Dartmouth student crested the hill, he heard thundering hoofs that could only mean a runaway horse.

On the other side of the hill, Paul Darrow was desperately attempting to control an animal spooked by a steam whistle. Yanking frantically on the reins, he managed to pull the horse up short. It reared and in coming down struck an object that Paul could not see.

Maguire raced to the scene and saw what his classmate could not. The frightened little boy had tried to run to his home across the street. Maguire picked up the stricken child. Harry's mother, Mrs. Arthur Cooley, was at the door. "I told her he would be alright, but I spoke untruthfully because I knew him to be dead," recalled the Dartmouth student.[2]

Returning to the street, Maguire found a shaken and inconsolable Paul Darrow. A doctor arrived shortly thereafter. A death certificate was completed that day: "Mother's maiden name: Laura M. Kendall; Cause and time of death: concussion of brain 3 PM; Age of deceased: 5 years, 3 months, 12 days." Peter Maguire said, "I never spoke of the accident to Paul, and he never spoke of it to me."[3]

On a June morning twenty-three years later the *Boston Globe*'s front page read "Lindbergh Quits His Hop to Paris" and "Chaplin Declares His Wife Untrue." But neither headline was as large as "Darrow May Go to Winters' Aid: Noted Chicago Lawyer to Keep Pledge Given by His Son Paul at Dartmouth 23 Years Ago, after Accident." The sensational story fed the public's insatiable appetite for news of Clarence Darrow's appearance in notorious cases.

America had been transfixed by "Darrow for the Defense" in each of the preceding three years. Saving Loeb and Leopold from execution in 1924 was followed by the "Scopes Monkey Trial" in 1925. A mesmerized country devoured news of Darrow's withering cross-examination of William Jennings Bryan for the famed orator's defense of Divine Creation. In 1926, Darrow successfully defended Ossian Sweet, a Black doctor accused of murder, when he and his family protected themselves from a mob enraged by their purchase of a house in a white neighborhood.

Reporters quickly established the link between Paul Darrow's 1904 letter to the bereaved mother of five-year-old Harry Cooley, and death row inmate John Winters. The boy's mother, Laura Kendall Cooley, was the sister-in-law of Maggie Cooley Winters, the mother of the convicted murderer.

The thirty-two-year-old Winters—a married factory worker and the father of three children—had been convicted of the first-degree murder of Cecelia Gullivan. Her mutilated body was found on the sleeping porch of her home on Monday morning November 8, 1926, by Frank Cone, Windsor's most prominent business leader.

In response to the obvious question—why hadn't Mrs. Cooley asked for Clarence Darrow's help in defending her nephew at the murder trial?—Winters' aunt replied she believed he was innocent and would not be convicted. It was a view many others shared. The State's evidence connecting her nephew to the murder was entirely circumstantial.

The murder of forty-three-year-old Cecelia Gullivan, an executive with the Cone Automatic Machine Company, shocked Vermonters. Thirty-six hours before the discovery of Gullivan's body, an intruder had broken into the home of Margaret "Tottie" Evarts and attacked her caregiver. "Murderous Attacks on Two Women Stir Windsor to High Pitch" headlined the *Vermont Tribune*. It characterized the death of Cecelia Gullivan as "the most brutal murder in the history of criminology in Vermont."[4]

The break-in was nearly as disturbing as the murder. Tottie Evarts was a thirty-four-year-old invalid living in a house that faced the stately residences of the "Evarts Estate." She was a descendant of William Maxwell Evarts, whose prominence in Windsor and American history had shaped the town's social and economic castes.

The combustible mix of an attack on a member of one of Vermont's most distinguished families, the brutality of the murder of Vermont's most prominent female executive, and "a public that lapped up tidings of lust and crime and cried for more," almost guaranteed what followed next.[5]

Within forty-eight hours, local authorities seized, but did not arrest, a suspect. While John Winters was being interrogated in the Windsor State Prison death cell, Vermont's governor announced the appointment of a special prosecutor. Newspapers from Boston to San Francisco reported murder in rural America "over wires jacked into the largest switchboard in the world."[6] President Calvin Coolidge, whose birthplace was thirty miles from Windsor and who had resisted having a telephone installed in his Plymouth Notch home, now saw dozens of reporters wiring the lurid details of the Vermont murder across the country.

Months before Clarence Darrow knew anything of the case, readers of metropolitan dailies and every Vermont newspaper formed conflicting and changing opinions about the strength of the State's case against John Winters. From a rush to judgment when initial disclosures seemed to point to guilt, to growing skepticism when prosecutors could find neither a murder weapon nor a witness, *State v. Winters* captured the public's fascination with crime.

The ingredients were there for the lapping. Small-town gossip cast suspicion on Frank Cone's relationship with Cecelia Gullivan—herself a figure of controversy merely by her business success as a single woman. But below the facile explanations lay the more disturbing ramifications of gender, class, and equal justice.

Cecelia Gullivan may have been murdered because of her gender. John Winters may have been prosecuted because he was an ex-convict. And when the special prosecutor was allowed by the judge to show to the jury the severed head of the victim, "presumption of innocence" became a meaningless phrase.

Clarence Darrow believed that the scales of justice were always stacked against a criminal defendant. Now—by accident—Paul Darrow had added the weight of America's most celebrated defense lawyer to John Winters' side of the scale.

⇒ 2 ⇐

Cecelia's Day

THE ROARING TWENTIES infused Windsor with an energy emblematic of the decade. President Calvin Coolidge was presiding over unprecedented economic growth—"Coolidge Prosperity," said his admirers. The Cone Automatic Machine Company prospered because of Frank Cone's innovative designs and the managerial expertise of Cecelia Gullivan.

In 1908, the forty-year-old manager of the Windsor Machine Company hired a bright, energetic young woman newly arrived from Massachusetts. Twenty-five-year-old Cecelia Gullivan was more than a breath of fresh air to a married father of three children. Her business acumen and efficiency became indispensable to Frank Cone as he confronted the pressure of managing a new industry in a new age.

Windsor was centered in "Precision Valley"—the name for the location of companies that comprised the foundation of the country's revolutionary modern machine tool industry. Despite its distance from easy transportation, raw materials, and centers of production, "Windsor seemed to have deliberately violated the laws of Economics."[1] The explanation was in part due to the remarkable confluence of inventive and mechanical genius that appeared to spring naturally from surrounding hillside farms.

The industry that propelled American material abundance had begun in Windsor when a gifted young mechanic, Richard Lawrence, joined Nicanor Kendall's gun-making shop. Together they devised a method for replicating rifle parts. In 1851, Lawrence and new partner Samuel Robbins brought their rifles with interchangeable parts to the Great Exhibition at London's Crystal Palace. Industrial and military leaders traveled to Windsor to see the "American System" of metalworking machines that "automatically" reproduced parts.[2]

When Frank Lyman Cone was born in 1868 six miles from Windsor, "automatic" was a word as new to most Americans as "computer" was to be a century later. But Cone—like the young programmers whose

7

innovations gave rise to the computer age—was literally on the cusp of a valley as significant to America's economic growth in the twentieth century as "Silicon Valley" is today.[3]

Frank Cone's aptitude for mechanical innovation was first demonstrated on his family's Weathersfield farm.[4] By 1895, when he began work at the Windsor Machine Company, precision machine tools were leading a new industrial revolution. Machine tools like lathes and drill presses were replicating standardized parts for myriad items from watches, bicycles, and sewing machines to engines and more.

George Gridley and Cone were tinkering with the invention of a multiple-spindle automatic lathe. Maxwell Evarts thought the new product so promising that he made a significant investment in the Windsor Machine Company and enticed others—including railroad baron Diamond Jim Brady—to do the same. "Dad was a great believer in Vermont," wrote his son Jeremiah. "He knew that anything produced in Vermont was superior to the same thing produced elsewhere."[5]

With the introduction of the four-spindle automatic "Gridley," business boomed. Frank Cone was managing a plant with more than 1,000 workers. Increasing demand for Windsor machines presented challenges. A new plant was part of the solution but lack of housing for hundreds of employees (almost all male) was a continuing dilemma. Maxwell Evarts, ill from cancer, sold his interest in the company in 1911, not long before his death.

An Ohio competitor, National Acme Company, bought Windsor Machine Company in 1916. NAMCO made some immediate changes. George Gridley was appointed manager and Frank Cone resigned.[6] Asked at trial for the date he left Windsor Machine Company, Cone replied, "We got done April 1, 1916."[7]

"We" meant he and Cecelia. Four months later, he started the Cone Automatic Machine Company. The first person Frank Cone hired was Cecelia Gullivan.

As Cone Automatic grew, so did Cecelia's authority. By 1926, the forty-three-year-old Gullivan had more responsibility for managing Cone Automatic than anyone except its owner. Her duties included—in addition to handling all finances as treasurer—requisitioning and pricing incoming orders for machines and tools. "She was a capable machine tool expert in her own right" asserted a knowledgeable observer of the industry.[8]

It was as rare to be a woman of consequence in Precision Valley's revolutionary machine tool industry as it was a century later to be a woman in the early days of Silicon Valley's computer revolution.[9] Charismatic with an "unusually wide circle of business acquaintances," Gullivan was a notable and recognizable Windsor resident.[10]

The fashions of the Roaring Twenties fit the slender Gullivan well: she was "an unusually attractive woman possessed of great personal charm," said an admirer.[11] She wore her hair bobbed and cut close to her head. She owned her own car. She built herself a new house. For many Windsor women—and men—Cecelia Gullivan was the new century's "modern woman."

Frank Cone spent as many as twenty days a month traveling by railroad between Windsor and Detroit, where "Conomatics" were widely used in Ford, General Motors, and Chrysler automobile manufacturing.[12] That meant that Gullivan was often on the floor of the Cone plant.

She frequently passed among the male machinists and tool makers, nearly all of whom she knew by name. Most Cone employees respected Gullivan because they understood that only Frank Cone had more authority, and because she clearly knew the business. Cecelia Gullivan knew something else as well—she knew what it was like to work with men.

The narrow clearance past the men in the tool department to her office was always challenging. The slim-waisted Gullivan was "just practically sideways, going through."[13] When comments were made, the remarks were audible over the machinery. "I would like to get next to her" may not have been heard by Gullivan, but a dozen men heard it. The worker added a visual. He humped a machine as she went past.

Cecelia Gullivan's house was her sanctuary. Described as "one of the prettiest in the village," the white bungalow with green shutters overlooked Windsor's Mill Pond.[14] Her decision to build a home of her own prompted local gossip. A rumor that she had been jilted by a man said more about a small town's need to explain why a successful single woman lived alone than it did about Cecelia.

A former roommate who knew of Cecelia's dream of owning a home and her financial discipline to achieve it, gave her a favorite pillow as a housewarming gift. To remind her, said her friend, of when Cecelia lived in more modest circumstances.

For Cecelia Gullivan, the first Saturday of November 1926 seemed as ordinary as the gray, 45-degree day Vermonters expect that time of year. She had slept, as was her custom, on the enclosed "sleeping porch" of the bungalow. Her active life was centered on her home and her job. The day promised rewards from each.

Saturday morning, Cecelia's attention was focused on yard work. A handyman, Alex Shambo, who often did work for her, stopped by to put the finishing touches on a box for the framing and planting of a rose garden. He knew that Cecelia was anxious that he finish by early afternoon.

Saturday evening, Cecelia expected to meet Frank Cone, who was returning from a business trip. In the owner's absence, Cecelia managed Cone Automatic. She knew that Cone would be interested in learning how business had been while he was gone. But that may not have been his only interest—nor hers.

Cecelia Gullivan's professionalism and pride in her job were reason enough to be attentive to how she looked when she was meeting her boss. Whether it was for that reason alone or not, on the evening of November 6 she took special care with her dress, hair, and shoes.

Cecelia's first stop was at Pond's barber shop at the corner of River and Main Streets. She arrived promptly at 8:30 p.m. for her appointment with John Young, Cecelia's stylist for the past five years. He cut the "boyish bob" she preferred, and Cecelia crossed the street to the Victory Cafe. Young noted her fashionable dress: "light with orange trimmings on the waist."[15]

Just after 9:00 p.m., Cecelia descended a few steps to George Patchis' shoe repair shop in the basement of the cafe, where she had left her shoes to be shined. Cecelia threaded her way through the pool room, Patchis' more lucrative cellar business. Two men were playing pool and a third was watching. She picked up her shoes and returned home to get ready for her visitor.

The married Cone lived a mile from Cecelia's house. At trial, Frank Cone was called by the State to testify about Cecelia Gullivan's responsibilities at Cone Automatic Machine Company. But prosecutors were concerned that defense lawyers might cross-examine the State's witness about a disquieting fact: Cone was at Cecelia's house after 11:00 p.m. on Saturday night.

The special prosecutor's anxiety was evident in the awkward question he asked in an effort to preempt the anticipated defense inquiry about why Cone was at her house at that hour:

Q. State whether or not you conferred about the matters concerning which you went up there to talk over?
A. Our whole conversation was business.[16]

Cone dared not deny—for fear that they had been seen—that he and Cecelia had taken a late Saturday night drive. It was, he said, "at her suggestion that we take the night air." Cone testified he was sure that he left

Cecelia at her home before midnight because he recalled winding his watch in his garage at 11:30 p.m.

When on cross-examination Winters' attorney asked, "What time was it when you went to Miss Gullivan's home on Sunday?" Cone was unsure. But this much was clear: the last person to see Cecelia Gullivan alive on Saturday night was Frank Cone. Sunday morning, she was dead.

⇒ 3 ⇐
Winters' Night

SATURDAY NIGHT IN A SMALL TOWN. John Winters was looking for liquor, women, and a card game. If that was incriminating conduct—as the State was to argue at trial—there were dozens of Windsor men whose evening would have been suspicious. But prosecutors had a more subtle objective in detailing Winters' activity on the night of November 6. They could account for his whereabouts until midnight but not after. And neither could John Winters.

It was easiest to find liquor. Prohibition had done no more to prevent the consumption of alcohol in Windsor, Vermont, than it had done anywhere else in America. Six years after the passage of the 18th Amendment, even Calvin Coolidge recognized that it was political dynamite to touch the issue. The president, said an observer, "remained at a safe distance and looked the other way."[1]

Like almost every other elected official, Coolidge said the law should be enforced. There was no shortage of opportunity. Vermont Attorney General J. Ward Carver was making headlines prosecuting a smuggler who killed a revenue agent who had interfered with rum running on Lake Champlain. Prosecutions for liquor violations provided more clients for defense lawyers. In Springfield, Vermont, attorneys Tupper and Bicknell were representing a prominent citizen whose open violation of Prohibition compelled local authorities to respond to the "drys" of the town.

In Windsor, the pastor of the Congregational Church condemned local authorities for making "no effort to check the sale of liquor." Speaking before the Rotary Club, he declared that Windsor was known as an "open town" where alcohol was easily obtained.[2] It is unlikely that was news to most Rotarians.

Clarence Darrow's well-founded belief that law and hypocrisy went hand and hand was repeatedly reinforced in the Roaring Twenties. Darrow, "as wet as the Flood," always knew where liquor could be found. Awaiting a verdict in a Detroit courthouse, he asked an obliging court officer to access the judge's Scotch supply.[3]

John Winters had his own sources. An "Italian fellow" on Central Street near the railroad tracks would sell a half pint of alcohol for $1.50. By adding water to reduce the potency, Winters then had a pint he could share with acquaintances as he ambled the streets on Saturday night. The practice was common enough to ensure that there would be a fellow worker to split the cost of the next half pint. Winters was to return to Central Street for alcohol more than once on the evening of November 6.

Winters started his night by bringing a bottle of wine from his house. His wife was certainly aware of her husband's drinking. But Winters, unlike his father, took care not to drink in front of his family. John Winters Sr. was convicted multiple times of alcohol violations when drinking was legal, but there is no record that his son ever was—even though the mere possession of liquor was a crime during Prohibition.

For liquor and cards—if not for women—Winters needed money. When he was a juvenile, he had taken a direct approach. Winters once entered a pool hall in Hanover, New Hampshire, asked for change for a quarter, struck the cashier with a bottle, and grabbed twenty dollars from the register. Witnesses said he escaped by swimming the Connecticut River to Vermont, where he was arrested.[4] "Excitable boy," they all said.

Thirty-two-year-old John Winters did not need to be so direct. Before starting his evening, Winters went to see a friend, Mary Chadbourne. He told her he needed money for a poker game with Dr. Ward. Mary gave him forty dollars. When asked why she had given Winters money, she responded, "why not?"

With cash in hand, Winters went to see Leslie Campbell: "He wanted me to get him into a card game in Windsor. Kind of a club. We have a room, just a few can go there." Winters had a soda bottle filled with wine that he took from under his couch at home. Campbell was unwilling to vouch for him though Winters had money. "I took a couple of drinks with him and that was the last I saw of him."[5] It was only 6:45 p.m.

At the corner of State and Main, Winters spotted George Putnam, who worked with him in the Cone Tool Department. Putnam was not interested in looking for a card game, but he told Winters that a "woman friend" might be arriving on the evening train. Winters said he knew someone on Central Avenue that would sell them a half pint of moonshine.

Winter and Putnam, half pint in hand, went to the train station but Putnam's friend did not arrive. Winters crossed the street where Mrs.

Stephanie Cole was standing in front of her store. He told her he had twenty dollars to spend on her if she was looking for a good time. "Not enough," replied Cole.

Putnam decided he would have better luck elsewhere without Winters. He told Winters that he was going to a Saturday night dance in Hartland five miles away. When Winters said he wanted to go with him, Putnam demurred. Putnam left him in front of the Victory Cafe. It was 9:00 p.m.

At 9:30 p.m. Winters was back on the street searching for more liquor and a card game. His 1917 Ford jalopy with a homemade truck bed remained on Main Street where he had parked it. He ambled up and down Windsor streets with an occasional foray to Central Avenue to purchase bootleg liquor.

By 11:00 p.m. Winters had shared soda bottles of moonshine with acquaintances and made at least one more stop at a co-worker's house. Otto Hochstein was willing to step outside to take a swig from Winters' bottle. Winters asked his fellow employee to join in the hunt for a card game. Mrs. Hochstein, awakened by the late-evening knock from a man who had never been to their house, did not embrace the idea.

Now, as midnight approached, Winters, "feeling pretty good," decided to drive to Hartland's Saturday night dance, where hours before his friend George Putnam had gone alone. When Winters arrived at the "English Garage" where the dance was held, there were no lights to be seen. Crossing back over an iron bridge, Winters stopped his car and went down an embankment in search of water.

Unsuccessful in his attempt to quench his thirst in Hartland, Winters drove back toward Windsor, stopping once at a watering trough. A quarter mile from his house, Winters parked his car at the Lamphere farm. There, he decided to steal apples. Finding that he had no bag to gather stolen apples, he drove home and awoke Sunday morning sick from his Saturday night of moonshine.

If that made no sense to a sober man, it was what Winters remembered. The risk of drinking homemade liquor during Prohibition was more than mere arrest. In New York, poisonous wood alcohol had killed and sickened hundreds. Liquor "purveyed by the neighborhood bootlegger" was dangerous, warned a *Rutland Herald* editorial: "After a night of aimless intoxication one could awaken as a prisoner charged with a brutal murder."[6]

⇒ 4 ⇐
Paradise

THE CONTRAST BETWEEN a nineteenth-century agricultural community and the automated industry propelling twentieth-century America was mirrored in the bucolic countryside surrounding Windsor. South from just above Hanover, the "Upper Valley" extended thirty miles downriver where the nation's longest covered bridge spanned the Connecticut River to link Cornish, New Hampshire, and Windsor, Vermont.

In Cornish, sculptor Augustus Saint-Gaudens was the focal point of a summer colony of artists and writers that blossomed to include an extended social circle on both sides of the river. The noted muralist Maxfield Parrish had a summer estate where the scenery mirrored an Italian landscape. Parrish crossed the bridge to do his banking in Windsor.[1]

Windsor residents were accustomed to notables. William Maxwell Evarts, who had been United States attorney general, secretary of state, and senator from New York, began his legal studies in Windsor. As his reputation grew, so did his acquisition of Windsor property. When in 1893 guests joined Evarts and his Windsor-born wife to honor their fiftieth wedding anniversary, the *New York Times* gushed, "Runnemede's grand old mansion and splendidly cultivated acres has been famous for hospitality that has been enjoyed by many of the most celebrated men and women of the century."[2]

Maxwell Evarts, youngest of the Evarts' twelve children, followed his father's footsteps as a lawyer and as Windsor's most prominent landholder. If Maxwell couldn't quite match the legal legacy of William Maxwell Evarts (whose brilliant closing argument to the United States Senate saved President Andrew Johnson from impeachment), he maintained the Evarts' preeminence in Windsor.

In 1902, Maxwell Evarts built a new mansion, designed by Augustus Saint-Gaudens, on Windsor's Juniper Hill. Several stately eighteenth-century homes along Windsor's North Main Street were added to the family's property portfolio. Two decades later, the compound of Evarts houses and its cultivated acreage (including the manmade Lake Runnemede) became a respite from urban life. Family members called it "Paradise."[3]

To a particular Evarts, whose editorial genius shaped the perception of American society in the Roaring Twenties, it "was the most glorious place on earth."[4] William Maxwell Evarts Perkins amplified the voice of a new literary generation when he championed F. Scott Fitzgerald's novels *This Side of Paradise* (1920) and *The Great Gatsby* (1925). "Max" Perkins came to Windsor as often as he could.

His mother Elizabeth, one of William Maxwell Evarts' twelve children, now owned a house in the Evarts family compound on North Main Street. Max Perkins' cousin, Margaret "Tottie" Evarts (daughter of Maxwell Evarts), lived across from the compound's homes. Once a vibrant girl who shared her father's love of horses and gift of winning ribbons when they rode together, thirty-four-year-old Tottie was now an invalid.

The cause of her disability was uncertain though often ascribed to "nervous disorder." Bessie Pandjiris had known Tottie as a healthy, active horsewoman with whom she had stayed at Juniper Hill Farm in 1923. Now, in 1926, Bessie was Tottie's nurse and full-time caretaker at an Evarts house on North Main Street.

On a Saturday night in November, Bessie, a housekeeper, and a cook followed a routine familiar to each other. Like each evening for the past few months, they went to bed after Miss Evarts was made comfortable. Bessie's bed was just a few feet from her charge's first-floor bedroom.

Shortly before 2:00 a.m. she was awakened by a faint cry. In the dim light, the nurse saw a man standing at the head of Tottie's bed. Upstairs, housekeeper Blanche Fowle awoke to the sound of gagging and quickly ran downstairs.

Bessie Pandjiris was on the floor in the middle of Tottie's room, her nightgown covered in blood. Next door, Walter and Elmer Moore were startled awake by the smash of glass. Someone could be heard running from the Evarts house. When Elmer Moore entered the Evarts house, he didn't at first recognize Tottie's nurse "because she looked as though she had been through a wreck."[5]

The housekeeper frantically called the police and a doctor. Windsor police, deputy sheriffs, and anxious neighbors descended upon the house. Bessie Pandjiris—her face swollen, eye blackened, and throat bruised—was unable to describe her assailant with specificity except to say that he smelled of liquor and had dirt on his hands and face.[6]

The battered nurse was put to bed. Blanche Fowle held the traumatized Tottie in her arms for the rest of the night. But before the housekeeper embraced Miss Tottie, she did one bit of cleaning. She picked some burrs from Bessie's blood-soaked nightgown and put them in an envelope.

$\Rightarrow$ 5 $\Leftarrow$

Murder!

Dr. Stoddard Martin looked forward to Sundays. To a man who lived alone in his office above the State National Bank on Windsor's Main Street, the highlight of his week was breakfast with Cecelia Gullivan. He had known her as a patient and friend for nearly twenty years. At 9:00 a.m., Sunday, November 7, Dr. Martin sat at their usual table at the Mirror Inn at the old Constitution House awaiting Cecelia's arrival. The punctual Gullivan was late.

It was unlike her, but Dr. Martin knew Cecelia well enough to respect her privacy—particularly on a Sunday morning. By 11:00 a.m. he was uneasy. News of the break-in and assault at the Evarts house was all over Windsor. But that was not why he went to her bungalow.

Dr. Martin was treating Cecelia for a condition she very much wished to keep private. He drove to her Clough Avenue home. The front door was locked but the doctor knew the house well and entered through an unlocked door on the north side. He stepped inside and hollered "Hello, Cecelia?"

Hearing no answer, Dr. Martin walked through "the little cozy dining room" and into the living room. Looking through the glass door to the sleeping porch, he saw nothing but a pile of clothes. He checked upstairs and the cellar without seeing a sign of Cecelia. Dr. Martin again called out "Cecelia?" but hearing no answer, he left.

Frank Cone twice went to Cecelia Gullivan's home on Sunday. At trial he was asked, "You have said that when you went to her home that Sunday morning, the first trip, you went to see her on business?" Cone answered, "Yes, business of importance." Asked about a second trip to her home that day, "Was that also business of importance?" Cone responded, "Yes, the same business."[1]

The contrast between Dr. Martin's search of the house for a sign of Cecelia and Cone's apparent disinterest may be explained by Dr. Mar-

18

tin's knowledge of Gullivan's medical condition. But Cone was more familiar with Cecelia's house than her doctor. If Cone's interest in seeing her was "business of importance," it was strange that he was not more diligent in looking for her on Sunday.

Cone's relative indifference as to Cecelia's whereabouts was particularly curious given the news of the break-in and assault at the Evarts house that was the talk of Windsor. By Sunday afternoon, Bessie Pandjiris was able to recount the night's trauma for reporters. Miss Tottie's nurse again said that because of the darkness she was unable to provide an accurate description of the man who attacked her, beyond her certainty that he had been drinking.

The traumatic events at the Evarts house dominated Sunday conversations of Windsor residents. At the Mirror Inn, Cecelia Gullivan's absence from Sunday afternoon dinner was little noted by other guests except Dr. Martin. "I thought," he later said, "that she had gone for a ride, perhaps, with someone."[2]

Frank Cone always began his workday at 8:00 a.m. Cecelia Gullivan was often there before him. On Monday morning, November 8, she was not. By 8:15 a.m. Cone was anxious enough about her absence to drive to her Clough Avenue house. This time he looked.

Peering through the sleeping porch window, Cone saw a foot sticking out of a bundle of clothes. When he walked to the north corner of the porch to get a better view, he saw Cecelia's mutilated head. Cone immediately drove to Dr. Martin's office, where the physician said they should go to the police station.

Accompanied by officers, they returned to the bungalow. Dr. Martin opened the door to the sleeping porch. A covered body lay on the bed. He lifted the cover to expose Cecelia's head, face, and neck. At trial, Dr. Martin was asked if he put the cover back after lifting it. "No," replied Cecelia's friend and physician: "I dropped the thing I was so horrified."[3]

Front-page stories in Boston erroneously reported that Cecelia Gullivan had a bullet wound to her head. Local newspapers noted that even "large metropolitan dailies" did not know if police had evidence or suspects. "Half the village population was divided on the issue of whether it was a case of murder or suicide," reported the *Vermont Tribune*. Frank Cone, according to the paper, "was at a loss to make a satisfactory explanation but said Miss Gullivan had been in a state of depression."[4]

Those who thought it was murder said that Miss Gullivan had been cautioned about the danger of sleeping on her enclosed porch during the summer and fall. The porch at the rear of Cecelia's house was "out of the hearing of neighbors"—another implicit suggestion that it was the lifestyle of a single woman that invited risk.

Hundreds of curious visitors drove to Cecelia's house hoping to see the gruesome murder scene. Some Windsor residents were eager to share rumors with reporters. The *Boston Globe* reported that investigators were searching for "love letters." Gossipers declared that shortly before the murder, Cecelia had said, "I have letters I must destroy." A lover jilted her and headed west twenty-four hours before she was killed, according to "wagging tongues."[5]

A titillated public awaited the release of the autopsy report. On Tuesday, November 9, the state's assistant medical examiner, Dr. Fred Kent, disclosed a partial summary of his findings. The "penetrating wound" was not caused by a gunshot. There were several additional deep cuts to the head and one across the bridge of the nose. There were bruises on the victim's throat and discolorations on her arms.

Two days later, over five hundred mourners gathered at the Church of the Holy Ghost in Whitman, Massachusetts, to pay their last respects to Cecelia Gullivan. "One of the most beloved and respected of Whitman's young women," read the *Brockton Daily Times*. It also reported that "President Cone of the firm with which Miss Gullivan was for nineteen years associated spoke feelingly to the heartbroken family." Cecelia's mother collapsed when she saw her daughter's body.[6]

Windsor County Sheriff Wallis Fairbanks and Windsor Chief of Police Bruce Degnan awaited the direction of Windsor County State's Attorney Robert Twitchell before continuing the investigation. But State's Attorney Twitchell was in Montpelier, where Attorney General J. Ward Carver had his own idea about who should lead the prosecution.

Carver became attorney general in May 1925 when Governor Franklin Billings appointed him to fill the vacancy created when the incumbent resigned. On November 2, 1926, Carver won his first election to the office. Now, a week later he was confronted with an unsolved murder that shocked Vermont and was front-page news across America.

Carver had been around long enough to know that the attorney general is not the best attorney in the office. Attorney General Carver was the only lawyer in his office. He needed a better prosecutor. The attorney general's request for a special prosecutor to lead the Gullivan murder case was quickly granted when Governor Billings learned who Carver was recommending.

Raymond J. Trainor was one of the best—some said *the* best—trial lawyers in Vermont. The forty-nine-year-old White River Junction attorney, "cocky, full of fight, and a master of strategy," built a practice on his reputation for winning difficult cases.[7] Trainor's trial skills were first recognized when as a young lawyer he was assigned by the court to defend an Italian immigrant accused of murder. Despite substantial evidence of guilt, the jury acquitted the defendant.

Windsor County voters decided to put Trainor on the State's side. In 1912 the thirty-four-year-old was elected Windsor County state's attorney. In one of his first trials as a prosecutor, a Windsor County jury returned a guilty verdict for rape twenty minutes after receiving the case.[8] State's Attorney Trainor had already secured guilty pleas from a youthful co-defendant.

The addition of the special prosecutor meant the office of attorney general was now composed of four persons: Trainor, Attorney General Carver, State Detective E. A. Brown, and a secretary. Unless the attorney general and special prosecutor intended to rely solely on the investigation of the crime by the Windsor County Sheriff's office and the Windsor Police Department, it was up to State Detective Brown to make the case.[9]

In a sensational murder case on the front pages of Boston and Vermont newspapers, Detective Brown knew prosecutors needed something more than evidence. They needed a suspect.

⇒ 6 ⇐
Prison Town

FOR A SMALL PROSPEROUS COMMUNITY with a history of distinguished citizenry and leaders of cutting-edge technology, Windsor's social divide was surprisingly deep. The reason was not difficult to divine. Windsor was a prison town, and by 1926 it had been one for over a century.

The idea that prisoners ought to be housed in a "state prison" that provided a modicum of humanity (regular meals, for example) was revolutionary. The selection of Windsor was a consolation prize when the legislature chose Montpelier as Vermont's capital instead of Windsor, where the state's constitution was drafted. At a time when Vermonters were struggling to carve a community out of wilderness, prison jobs were a blessing.[1]

Constructed of stone quarried from nearby Mt. Ascutney, the prison's walls were fourteen feet high and three feet thick. It opened in 1809 on land sold to the town by one of Windsor's most prominent citizens, Stephen Jacob, who had served on the Vermont Supreme Court from 1801–1802. It is doubtful that Windsor got the best of Justice Jacob, who had a history of protecting his purse.

In 1783, Jacob purchased thirty-year-old Dinah from a Connecticut slave trader. Seventeen years later, Justice Jacob turned her out on the street, "infirm, sick, and blind." The Town of Windsor, now responsible for her care as a pauper, sued Jacob for Dinah's upkeep.

The opinion of Chief Justice Royall Tyler in *Selectmen of Windsor v. Jacob* is celebrated because it declared slavery unconstitutional in Vermont. But it was really a decision to protect Justice Jacob. By declaring slavery unconstitutional, his fellow justices held that the town's proof of slavery (a bill of sale showing Justice Jacob bought a slave) could not be admitted as evidence. Without proof that Jacob was responsible for Dinah, he had no obligation to the town for her sustenance. The Vermont Supreme Court awarded court costs to Justice Jacob.[2]

Serving a private interest at the expense of the public was apparent in the history of the prison as well. A century later, Windsor State Prison conditions were as subject to the character of its warden as any other of the country's now ubiquitous state prison systems. Superintendent Edwin Oakes arranged to feed his Lake Sunapee cottage guests the best food public money could buy. Inmates were served maggot-infested beef.

A legislative investigation uncovered more malfeasance, including the practice of allowing private citizens to "hire" inmates. The superintendent's brother used prison labor to raise vegetables, which he then sold to the prison. Prison guards frequently had convicts doing chores around their own homes.[3]

One result of the 1905 prison scandal, in addition to the removal of Superintendent Oakes, was the creation of a system of accountable prison labor. Within the prison, inmates could make shirts for the Reliance Shirt Company under contract with the state. Outside the massive prison walls, convicts could work on a farm of 300 acres—sold to the state by Maxwell Evarts.

By 1916, new Superintendent R. H. Walker reported that "the number of men working on the farms is steadily increasing and this work is an incentive to good conduct." Of the 217 inmates, thirty-six were serving time for burglary, the most common reason for incarceration. Nearly as many, twenty-nine, were serving time for adultery. Sixteen inmates were serving time for rape and three for statutory rape.[4]

John Winters was serving time for both. He was to later claim that the prosecutor was spurred by vindictive fathers of young women who had engaged in consensual sex, but in January 1913 eighteen-year-old Winters entered guilty pleas to one count of rape and one count of statutory rape.[5] Before the month ended, Winters was serving a twelve-to-fifteen-year sentence that could keep him incarcerated until 1928.

Winters attempted to escape during his first year of imprisonment. Reports that he had done so were corrected by prison authorities sensitive to public criticism after a series of breakouts. They declared that Winters had been found hiding in the prison workshop with a ladder and "overpowered."[6]

Despite his attempted escape, John Winters' conduct during the next five years was good enough to make him a candidate for release before completing his maximum sentence. On Christmas Eve 1919, he was released from Windsor State Prison after serving six years.

Winters' release posed the same dilemma a prison town always faced: how best to integrate into society an individual who has served his time.

The problem was particularly acute in a town as small as Windsor. "It is asking too much of one community to absorb so many of these men," editorialized the *Vermont Journal*. The newspaper proposed a law "which would remove Windsor from being the dumping ground for many of the convicts whose terms expire at the State Prison." But even it conceded that ex-convicts "have gotten along well in the majority of cases."[7]

John Winters was an example of that majority. He had good reasons to make a new life in Windsor. His mother moved from Rutland to Windsor to be closer to her incarcerated son. She shared an apartment with her daughter Anna (John's sister) in "The Block"—tenement housing newly constructed by NAMCO, the company that had bought the Windsor Machine Company in 1916.[8]

Maggie Winters was a laundress and cook for assorted members of the Evarts family. She told her son that she could find him work on the Evarts estate. Winters did odd jobs on the Juniper Hill farm. He caned some chairs for Margaret "Tottie" Evarts.

On Valentine's Day 1920, twenty-five-year-old John Winters married Mabel Sargent, the eighteen-year-old daughter of Mr. and Mrs. George Sargent of Windsor. The Winters' first child, a daughter, died after a premature birth in July. But in August of the following year, a son, John Albert Winters, was born.

Winters kept busy working at Juniper Hill. His one-year-old son was doted over by his in-laws and his mother. The child was of special interest to John's uncle, Arthur Cooley, and his wife, who had no son since the death of little Harry Cooley, fifteen years before.

In November 1922, tragedy again struck the extended Winters-Cooley family when fifteen-month-old John Albert Winters died of acute meningitis. The impact of the loss touched even the Evarts family. Tottie Evarts paid for the funeral of the child.

In 1923 the couple had a new son. They named him "Arthur"—a sign of the closeness of John Winters to his uncle and Mrs. Arthur Cooley. Another boy was born a year later. "John is a good father, passionately devoted to his children," said his wife, Mabel.[9]

The Winters moved into a partially completed house on the Windsor fairgrounds. John scrabbled together building materials including lumber and tools, some donated to him by Frank Cone. John Winters was clapboarding his house on Sunday, November 7, 1926, when the police came.

⇒ 7 ⇐

A Suspect

THE *VERMONT TRIBUNE* put the state's investigative approach more directly than prosecutors would have preferred: "Windsor Village has the Vermont State prison. Each day that passes sees the release of prisoners whose terms of confinement are up. Some of these men are of the lowest type. Those in charge of the preliminary investigation thought that here was the solution to the mystery of the murder."

The *Tribune* continued: "So the name of John Winters was selected as a person who ought to be held for examination." The newspaper added, "He is married and so far, has kept out of trouble. In this instance he was not even under arrest." But investigators had placed him in the prison "for safe keeping until he could be given an examination."[1]

If prosecutors were displeased with investigators sharing the reason that Winters was viewed as a suspect, they must have been apoplectic at Wallis Fairbanks. The Windsor County sheriff told the *Rutland Herald* that John Winters would soon confess to murder because "he will not be able to bear up under the cruel grilling to which he has been subjected by State Detective E. A. Brown."[2]

Sheriff Fairbanks made more front-page news by asserting that there was little doubt that Winters was guilty of the break-in at the Evarts house. Fairbanks added he was confident that Miss Tottie's nurse, Bessie Pandjiris, would identify Winters as the man who assaulted her. The Windsor County sheriff appeared to have solved the case.

Wallis Fairbanks needed favorable press coverage. Less than a week before the murder of Cecelia Gullivan, Sheriff Fairbanks was sentenced to not less than two years in Windsor State Prison for having sexual relations with two young women who were wards of the state. The sheriff's trial included evidence that Fairbanks "had sexual intercourse in the pine woods in Rockingham on an occasion when the other girl was present."[3]

The married sheriff was convicted of a "statutory charge." Although newspapers would print the names and ages of rape victims, they would not use the word adultery. Twenty-one-year-old unmarried Irma Stoodley, who testified about her relationship with Sheriff Fairbanks, was sentenced to another year in Rutland's Riverside Reformatory.

Fairbanks was reelected sheriff of Windsor County on the same day the jury returned its guilty verdict. At sentencing, he asked for leniency "for the sake of my wife and daughter."[4] His sentence was stayed pending his appeal to the Vermont Supreme Court. Fairbanks was released on $3,000 bail. One week later, the convicted sheriff was at Windsor Prison interrogating John Winters—who had not even been arrested.

State Detective Brown did not care if Fairbanks took credit when John Winters was arrested, if the Windsor County sheriff stayed out of the experienced Brown's way. For an arrest Brown needed evidence—unless, of course, Winters confessed. The prison warden told the attorney general's investigator that Winters could be a "tough nut."[5] Brown believed he could crack one.

On Monday afternoon of November 8—the day the body was discovered—officers went to John Winters' house. He was taken to Windsor Prison and put in the death cell. He was not told why he was taken. On Monday evening, Winters was brought to the warden's office. State's Attorney Robert Twitchell, Detective Brown, Windsor Police Chief Bruce Degnan, and other officers were already there.

. They brought with them a pair of trousers that had been on a chair in Winters' home. Winters was later asked with whom he had talked. "They all had something to say to me," said Winters, "Mr. Brown more than the rest."[6] Winters was asked: How did you get blood and burrs on your trousers? What caused the tear in the pants? Winters said he didn't know.

Winters was confined in Windsor State Prison for the next five days. He was kept in the death cell because—according to the warden—it was more comfortable and larger than other cells. It was also a useful venue to apply the "good cop/bad cop" interrogation technique. Detective Brown played both parts.

During the extended questioning Monday evening, Brown at one point asked Winters to step into the bathroom. "He told me he was a father of boys like me, and he felt sorry for me and would help me out. He told me he was the man to tell it to if I did it."[7] When Winters denied having anything to confess, Detective Brown reverted to bad cop. He told him that a handful of Winters' hair was in Cecelia Gullivan's hand.

Prosecutors had no such evidence. They had no witnesses who could place John Winters at Gullivan's house on the early morning of November 7 when she was murdered. They had not found a murder weapon. Investigators did not know what the murderer had used to kill Cecelia.

"More than a score of Boy Scouts scoured the lawns around the Gullivan house in the hope of finding some weapon with which the murder was accomplished," reported the *Rutland Herald.*[8] An attempt to drain Mill Pond next to the Gullivan bungalow in the hope of finding evidence was abandoned because of high water and the muddy bottom. But twelve-year-old Eugene Bulkington and friends were examining icicles at the Mill Pond Dam when under the float next to the dam, he saw the edge of a pillow.

"I told my mother, but she didn't believe me,"[9] Eugene said. With a skeptical mother in tow, he returned to the pond. Eugene jumped from the dam to the float and pulled up the pillow. The pillowcase was still on but there was a tear in it. Eugene noticed something else: there were big stains on the case that made it stick to the pillow.

By the second day of Winters' interrogation, Detective Brown recognized that the case and Winters were tough nuts to crack. It was obvious to the attorney general's investigator that a suspect in the break-in and assault at the Evarts house would be a prime suspect in the murder case.

Indeed, on Tuesday morning, newspapers were reporting that an important clue in the murder case could be the statement of Mrs. Bessie Pandjiris, the nurse who was caring for Miss Evarts. Pandjiris had told reporters immediately after the assault that she could not describe her assailant because of the darkness. Detective Brown believed he could remedy that problem.

On Tuesday evening, Brown, accompanied by other officers, brought Winters to the Evarts house. Once there, he instructed Winters to stand at the head of Miss Tottie's bed and whisper the words "diamonds, jewels, and money" while looking down at the bed-ridden invalid. Brown placed the nurse where she had been that evening, a few feet from the bed.

Five minutes later, Detective Brown took John Winters into the kitchen of the Evarts house and told him that Bessie Pandjiris had identified him as her assailant. Winters did not believe him: "I want to hear that from her own lips." When Mrs. Pandjiris told Winters, "You are the man who was in here," Winters exclaimed, "I hope to die if it was me. Take me out and hang me!"[10]

Armed with the Pandjiris statement, Brown was sure that he could persuade Winters to admit to the Evarts house break-in—an admission that would give the State its murder suspect. "For God's sake, John, if you have done this, I want you to tell me," Brown said to him.[11] Winters said he had nothing to admit.

Detective Brown's difficulty in building a case was not reflected in news coverage. Newspapers had already convicted John Winters. During the week Winters was being interrogated, Sheriff Fairbanks provided reporters with damning information that had little to do with actual evidence. Winters' "unsavory record" was emphasized as was an unproven (and uncharged) claim by a woman who said Winters had tried to assault her in her brother's house.

The sheriff was never reluctant to offer his opinion, declaring that there was little doubt that Winters would be convicted of the crimes at the Evarts house and face fifteen to twenty-five years in prison—and the electric chair if a murder charge was proven.

The problem—among others—of first convicting John Winters in the press was that he had not yet been arrested. On the fifth day of the suspect's confinement for interrogation, Detective Brown informed Special Prosecutor Raymond Trainor that he ought to come to the prison to see if together they might get a signed admission of some kind from the weary Winters.

Trainor arrived at Windsor State Prison on Friday evening, November 12. The *Vermont Standard* reported that "Trainor and others went to the death cell where Winters was confined and grilled him concerning his movements on the night when the crime was committed. Mr. Trainor came away with a signed statement which is thought to be tantamount to a confession."[12]

It was time for Sheriff Wallis Fairbanks to make an announcement. On Saturday, November 13, with John Winters "standing in the death-house, beside the electric chair where his soul may be hurled into eternity in answer for his crime," the sheriff read three warrants. Winters was accused of breaking and entering the Evarts house with intent to rob; attempted assault of Bessie Pandjiris; and the murder of Cecelia Gullivan. "Did the statement I signed last night have anything to do with this?" Winters quietly asked.[13]

The statement was signed by Winters in the presence of Special Prosecutor Trainor and Detective Brown after five days of interrogation in the Windsor prison death cell. It was far from being "tantamount to a confession."

Defense lawyers were later to unsuccessfully argue that the State coerced Winters into signing the statement. Trainor and Brown contended that they had offered to get their suspect an attorney. According to the attorney general's prosecutor and detective, Winters had replied, "What in hell good would a lawyer do me now?"

But Winters insisted—despite being pressed by Special Prosecutor Trainor—that he was not advised he could have a lawyer until *after* he signed the statement:

> Q. (Trainor): Were you told by Mr. Brown at least twice that evening that you ought to have a lawyer?
> A. (Winters): No.
> Q. Did you reply when told you ought to have a lawyer, "What in hell good will a lawyer do me?"
> A. Yes, after I signed the statement when you told me I was entitled to a lawyer.[14]

The timing of the offer remained in dispute. But when John Winters was charged with murder and could not afford a lawyer, the court assigned him one. Detective Brown's attempt to save the State the trouble of a jury trial failed. The special prosecutor and the detective had miscalculated: either Winters really was a tough nut—or worse—he was not the murderer.

⇒ 8 ⇐

Game On

HERBERT TUPPER WAS A LAWYER with a general practice in Springfield, Vermont, fifteen miles from Windsor. John Winters was fortunate that the Springfield attorney was chosen to defend him. Tupper was not Clarence Darrow, but he was good enough to earn Darrow's admiration, who held him in such high regard that they became friends after working together on Winters' appeal.[1]

On Monday, November 15, Tupper went immediately to Windsor prison where Winters was still being held. The State intended to arraign Winters the next day on each of the three crimes in Sheriff Fairbanks arrest warrants: breaking and entering the Evarts house with intent to rob; the assault on Miss Tottie's nurse, Bessie Pandjiris; and the murder of Cecelia Gullivan.

The arraignment was for the purpose of formally charging Winters with the crimes and for entry of a plea. Prosecutors anticipated Winters would initially plead not guilty—though others including Fairbanks and readers of newspaper accounts may well have expected Winters to admit all. His defense attorney had a different plan.

After spending several hours with Winters, Herbert Tupper announced that his client would not enter a plea but would instead compel the State to demonstrate at the hearing that it had enough evidence to support the arrests. If John Winters is to be charged with murder, upon what evidence has the arrest been made, his attorney wanted to know.

It was a good question. Special Prosecutor Raymond Trainor knew he could not answer it. The State asked that the hearing be postponed for a week. Tupper requested the court to at least compel the prosecutor to offer evidence to support the breaking-and-entering and assault charges. Trainor replied that Mrs. Bessie Pandjiris was ill—the first of three instances when "illness" was remarkably good fortune for the prosecution.

The State's failure to produce any evidence at the hearing stunned Windsor residents—to say nothing of *Boston Globe* readers—who had been led to believe that Winters had all but confessed to murder. "Popular indignation against Winters subsides," the *Globe* reported the next day, noting that "many persons think that Winters might have been intoxicated but he is not guilty of the crimes attributed to him by the authorities."[2]

The authorities were now scrambling to save an investigation that had been upended by defense attorney Tupper. As Special Prosecutor Trainor and Detective E. A. Brown well knew, the puzzle of who murdered Cecelia Gullivan was missing some big pieces: a witness and a murder weapon.

Beyond the challenge of constructing a murder case against Winters that would be entirely circumstantial, the attorney general's representatives were hampered by the incompetence of Windsor County's chief law enforcement authorities: State's Attorney Robert Twitchell and Sheriff Wallis Fairbanks.

Fairbanks, a shameless self-promoter (and convicted felon), was largely responsible for the notoriously prejudicial stories that had all but convicted Winters in the press. Twitchell, to whom Trainor had deferred in conducting the initial inquest, was so inept in questioning witnesses that the special prosecutor called many of them again and reexamined them himself.

The postponement of the preliminary hearing until November 23 may have given the State more time to get its act together, but it also provided a week in which the public perception of Winters was altered. Reporters, now skeptical of the Sheriff Fairbanks version of Winters and the evidence, presented a more nuanced portrayal of the defendant.

Several newspapers asserted that Winters had friends that were helping him fight the charges. Not only were his mother and wife visiting him daily in prison, many others were as well. When a story instigated by Fairbanks claimed Winters was near a nervous breakdown, it was quickly refuted by friends of Winters who said he was calmly awaiting his day in court.[3]

"Calm" was not the appropriate adjective to describe residents of Windsor as the day of the preliminary hearing approached. Speculation that the murderer could have been a jilted lover was fueled by references in articles to missing "love letters" that were purportedly on Gullivan's bed stand when her body was found.

And, ever since the *Boston Evening Globe*'s March 13 banner headline across eight columns, "New Turn in Investigation of Woman Murder in Vermont" with the subline, "Victim's Auto Ride Saturday Night Being Investigated," more than a few in Windsor wondered what Frank Cone would have to say for himself.

But before there could be answers to questions about evidence, charges, or suspects, the *Rutland Herald* posed another question: where could the November 23 hearing be held? The *Herald* noted that "several small halls which have been mentioned are considered altogether too small for the crowds which are expected to flock to one of the most sensational cases ever to be held in this state."[4]

Those in charge of locating a larger hall chose the cavernous State Armory. Windsor locals knew it as "Home of the Yellowjackets," the Windsor High School basketball team. Doors were opened early to accommodate the hundreds who rushed to fill seats around the basketball court.

Tables had been placed in the middle of the court. Presiding Judge R. Ward Dent sat at one. Another larger table was filled by reporters from Vermont, Boston, and other city newspapers. At one counsel table in the tip-off ring, Special Prosecutor Trainor could be seen making notes. At the other, defense attorney Tupper sat awaiting the arrival of his client.

With the sudden opening of a large heavy armory side door, the murmurs grew so loud that Judge Dent called for order in the court—a directive easier to enforce in a courtroom than on a basketball court. Sheriff Fairbanks and prison guards escorted John Winters past courtside spectators straining for a view of the defendant.

John Winters did not look like the crowd thought a murderer should look. His complexion was fair and clean shaven. His build was slim and of average height. He wore pressed gray trousers and a collared white shirt, with a neatly knotted black tie. Winters "looked more like a dreamer than a man capable of crime."[5]

Defense attorney Tupper was the first to rise at mid-court. "Mr. Winters has been confined for more than two weeks in the Windsor Prison death cell. Suspicion of murder is not a basis for holding him. It is not a basis for arresting him without evidence. What is the evidence?" It was game on.

Special Prosecutor Trainor replied that while the State was prepared to offer evidence to support the arrest of Winters for the assault on Bessie Pandjiris—the nurse having recovered from her previous "indisposition"—the State could not at this hearing present evidence related to a charge of murder. "Why not?" asked Winters' lawyer. "Because," replied Trainor, "Detective Brown is ill."

Defense attorney Tupper was immediately on his feet. "Your Honor, I ask leave to call Sheriff Fairbanks to the stand." "For what purpose?"

asked Judge Dent. "To demonstrate that the Sheriff and Mr. Brown were recently in conversation and the attorney general's investigator showed no symptoms of illness," replied Tupper.

The court denied Tupper's request. Trainor knew that a judge who favors the prosecution is even better than a weak excuse. Defense attorney Tupper could not resist a remark that amused the spectators more than the court: "Perhaps Detective Brown has gone to Maine for Thanksgiving."[6]

Tupper argued that the prosecution should not be allowed to present evidence of the assault on Miss Tottie's nurse unless the State was also prepared to present evidence on the murder charge. Judge Dent allowed the special prosecutor to proceed. Bessie Pandjiris was fully recovered from her "illness."

Mrs. Pandjiris was an imposing figure who spoke "like a trained elocutionist."[7] Her dramatic recounting of the assault in the Evarts house mesmerized spectators who overcame their disappointment at not hearing murder evidence. For a witness who was unable to provide an identification of her assailant in the first forty-eight hours after the assault, she was now remarkably certain of who attacked her.

Q. (Trainor): Did John Winters assault you?
A. (Pandjiris): Yes.
Q. Are you positive in your identification?
A. Yes.
Q. Any doubt about it?
A. No.[8]

Listeners riveted by the nurse's dramatic account of her struggle with her assailant did not notice a prosecutorial question that troubled Tupper. When the defense attorney heard Bessie Pandjiris' answer to the prosecutor's question, "What if anything did you find in your bed sheets after the assault," Tupper realized that her answer, "burrs," was not evidence needed for an assault charge.

Judge Dent ruled there was probable cause for the arrest of Winters on the charge of assault. Attorney Tupper successfully argued that the State's request for $25,000 bail was excessive, but it was a pyrrhic victory because Winters was not entitled to bail if the murder charge remained.

The defense attorney's greater success was in persuading the court to set a December 1 hearing at which the State would be compelled to present what evidence, if any, it had to hold John Winters for the murder of Cecelia Gullivan.

As the armory emptied, the defendant's mother approached her son and kissed him affectionately. It was, many noticed, the first time in the ordeal that John Winters became emotional. Sheriff Fairbanks and prison guards marched their prisoner back to the death cell.

The confinement was beginning to tell on Winters. His mother could see he was thinner. On December 1, when Winters was again brought from the death cell for a hearing to determine whether the State had sufficient evidence to charge him with murder, others observed his weight loss and dark circles about his eyes.

As before, spectators filled the seats. Reporters particularly noted, without speculating about the reason, "hundreds of women filling the long tiers of chairs along the sides of the hall."[9] Judge Dent, reporters, and defense attorney Tupper again sat at tables in the middle of the basketball court. Winters could be seen speaking in low tones to his lawyer as they awaited the arrival of Special Prosecutor Trainor.

He did not appear. Windsor State's Attorney Twitchell, seated at the prosecutors' table, explained to the court that Trainor had apparently been delayed. Then, as an impatient judge demanded a reason for the prosecutor's tardiness, Twitchell replied, "Mr. Trainor is ill."

The state's attorney, to whom a note had just been passed, added, "Your Honor, the State asks that the initial charges filed against John Winters for breaking and entering into the Evarts House with intent to rob, and for the murder of Cecelia Gullivan be dismissed." Judge Dent asked, "Does the State also wish to dismiss the charge of assault on Bessie Pandjiris?" Twitchell responded, "No."[10]

Special Prosecutor Trainor's illness may have been contrived, but as with the equally spurious maladies of Bessie Pandjiris and Detective Brown, one result was certain: the defendant stayed in prison. John Winters remained what he had been since November 9: a suspect, neither arrested nor charged in the death of Cecelia Gullivan.

Trainor was playing a deep game. Still unable to provide enough evidence at the December 1 preliminary hearing to link Winters to the murder of Cecelia Gullivan, the prosecution dismissed the murder charge (and the charge of breaking and entering with intent to rob) so the State could convene a grand jury.

Grand juries are seldom used in Vermont. There had not been one in Windsor County for five years. But a grand jury has two enormous advantages for prosecutors: it is conducted in secret, and defense attorneys are not permitted to attend. The oft quoted aphorism "a grand jury would indict a ham sandwich" has more than a grain of truth.[11]

Special Prosecutor Trainor began his presentation of evidence to the grand jury on December 8. Although conducted in secrecy, reporters learned that the State would be seeking an indictment for murder in the first degree; fifty-three witnesses would be called; and testimony would take several days.

On December 16, 1926, the grand jury indicted John Winters for the murder of Cecelia Gullivan in the first degree and for the assault of Bessie Pandjiris. Winters pleaded not guilty to each count the next day. He was returned to the Windsor Prison death cell, "the place he has called home for the last six weeks more unperturbed than ever." Winters' attorneys were said to be laying a "mighty campaign" for his acquittal.[12]

Sheriff Wallis Fairbanks had no doubt about the outcome. When questioned by reporters, Fairbanks laughed at the idea of an acquittal, adding "we have had an iron-bound case against Winters from the beginning."[13] An "iron-bound case" would include a murder weapon. If authorities had found one, the sheriff would have been the first to leak the news to the press.

Special Prosecutor Trainor believed he had something more compelling to show a jury than a murder weapon: Cecelia Gullivan's head.

⇒ 9 ⇐

The State's Case

THE TRIAL OF JOHN WINTERS for the murder of Cecelia Gullivan began on January 19, 1927. Seating was at a premium in the simple, classic Woodstock courthouse. Prospective jurors were jostled by spectators and reporters vying for space. Those "from away" were surprised to see three judges on the bench. A practice unique to Vermont provided lay "side judges" to assist the presiding trial judge.[1]

The judge that counted was Frank Thompson, who had been a trial judge for only four years. Previously a reporter of decisions for the Vermont Supreme Court, Thompson had served as state's attorney for both Caledonia and Orleans counties. The State correctly anticipated that Thompson would favor the prosecution more than the defense.

The prosecutorial team at the Windsor County courthouse for jury draw on the morning of January 19 was a "team" in name only. State's Attorney Robert Twitchell was included solely because the case was being tried in his county. Attorney General J. Ward Carver had two insights that can serve an ambitious attorney general well. First, choose a good lawyer to try the case. Second, be on hand to take credit if the case goes well.

The prosecutor that mattered was Special Prosecutor Raymond Trainor. As the defense was soon to learn, Trainor had two qualities that made him one of Vermont's leading trial lawyers: he was painstaking in his preparation, and he was a master of cross-examination.

Defense attorney Herbert Tupper was joined by attorney Fred Bicknell. If the State intended to call even half as many witnesses as the fifty that testified before the grand jury, Tupper would need help. But co-counsel Bicknell's help would be devastating to the defense of John Winters.

Maggie Winters accompanied her son to and from prison to the courtroom. John Winters sat with his mother during each court recess. "This quiet appearing chap appears to be what his mother says he is—a good, devoted son," said an observer.[2] Seated with his mother every day of the trial was the defendant's aunt, Laura Cooley.

When Special Prosecutor Trainor rose to address the jury on the cold winter's morning of January 21, he began, "Gentlemen of the jury." Women were not permitted to serve on Vermont juries until 1943.[3] The jury was largely composed of farmers.

Clarence Darrow may have been thinking of the Winters jury when on the eve of his argument to the Vermont Supreme Court he told Norwich University cadets: "On juries before which I appear I don't want any hard-working farmers whose sole pleasure in life is church attendance on Sunday. Sympathetic, imaginative jurors who can laugh and cry are the kind I want."[4]

Awaiting an opening statement that would at last reveal how the State intended to prove beyond a reasonable doubt a murder case based solely on circumstantial evidence, all eyes were on the prosecutor. It may have been the moment that John Winters realized that the man who sent him to prison for rape was Raymond Trainor.

Trainor was full of surprises. His claims of illness to delay hearings when there was insufficient evidence to charge Winters with murder were made to give the prosecution time to build a circumstantial case. In an era when prosecutors were not required to disclose evidence to the defense prior to trial, Winters' lawyers had little more knowledge of the State's case than the spectators in the courtroom.

The special prosecutor cleverly made it sound to the jury like he was outlining the case as a favor to the defense: "I make this opening statement for two purposes: First, in order that you gentlemen may more easily understand the evidence as it is introduced, and second, that the defendant and his counsel get an idea of the evidence that the State has."[5]

For one hour, attentive jurors and a rapt audience listened as the prosecutor spun a narrative of "little links" that he said could have only one ending: "a long chain of circumstantial evidence all linked together to point conclusively to but one man who did this terrible murder—that man is this defendant, John C. Winters."

Trainor knew that the relative proximity of Winters' home, Gullivan's bungalow, and the Evarts house (all within a mile and a half of each other) was evidence of—if nothing else—Winters' opportunity to commit the crime. Although a defendant has no burden to prove his innocence, the prosecutor was not above suggesting otherwise to the jury: "The State will introduce evidence of the defendant's utter inability to account for his whereabouts after midnight."

The evidence tended to show that the murderer had entered Gullivan's house by removing a cellar window that was found in the bushes below the house. Trainor contended the murderer had left the house by going through the backyard and across the Mill Pond dam that was below the bungalow. The most direct route to John Winters' house was across the Mill Pond dam.

To get to the dam, one had to go through a barbed wire fence. The bloody pillow from Cecelia Gullivan's bed found tucked under the float by twelve-year-old Eugene Bulkington had a tear consistent with being pricked by a barbed wire strand. The trousers Winters wore on the night of November 6 were torn and had blood on them.

But Trainor had another objective in emphasizing evidence that the murderer had broken into Gullivan's home. It lessened the possibility that the defense could lead jurors to think that Frank Cone was a suspect. Cone would not have had to break in.

Special Prosecutor Trainor's skillful opening argument was revealing in what it contained—and what it did not. Although it is not necessary for the State to prove a murderer had a motive, Trainor knew the impact the testimony of Winters' co-workers would have on jurors: "The State will introduce evidence from the lips of his friends that Winters had a lustful desire for Miss Gullivan, a desire to have sexual intercourse with her."

The State's opening may have persuaded jurors and spectators that Winters had motive and opportunity—and no alibi—but what had the murderer used to kill Cecelia Gullivan? For the first time in his opening statement, Trainor did not refer to the murder victim as Miss Gullivan nor as the "murdered woman."

The special prosecutor said, "The State will show you what kind of weapons *this girl* was killed with" (emphasis added). Trainor was too experienced to have made an inadvertent slip. He then added a disclaimer the jury must have found puzzling: "Of course, the State won't show you the weapon or weapons that must have killed her. But the State will show you two weapons that, owing to the peculiar nature of the wounds on this girl's head, neck, and face *could* have made the wounds" (emphasis added).

What the prosecution knew, and the defense did not, was that when investigators were unable to find a murder weapon, Special Prosecutor Trainor built the circumstantial case around a chisel and a steel spring taken from Winters' house one week after the murder. The State's medical expert, prepped by the prosecutor, would testify that the instruments fit the wounds.

But the State's opening argument was also an indication of how difficult it would be to prove beyond a reasonable doubt that Winters murdered Cecelia Gullivan, without introducing evidence of the Evarts house break-in and assault of Bessie Pandjiris.

The prosecutor referred to footprints and blood stains in Gullivan's bungalow. In fact, the State was never able to find blood or footprint evidence that irrefutably tied Winters to the murder. Detective E. A. Brown told Winters that Winters' hair was found in Cecelia Gullivan's hand. Special Prosecutor Trainor never mentioned hair at all.

Trainor told the jury they would be given microscopes to examine the similarities between dirt found in the cuffs of Winters' trousers and in the victim's bedroom. But the strength of that argument depended on whether the jurors believed that Sheriff Wallis Fairbanks properly preserved the evidence.

More damning were "burrs" found by Miss Tottie's housekeeper after the assault at the Evarts house. In his opening statement, the special prosecutor was prepared to go as far as the court would allow in linking Winters to that crime: "The State will introduce evidence to show that about ten minutes after two on that Sunday morning, this defendant was in the home of Miss Tottie Evarts." Defense Attorney Tupper immediately objected.

Judge Thompson agreed it was improper for the State to talk about the Evarts house crime until the court decided whether the evidence from the events of that night was relevant to the murder charge. "I think it would be better to omit the details," Thompson told the prosecutor.

The judge did not have to determine whether the State could introduce evidence related to the Evarts house break-in and assault until Trainor called Bessie Pandjiris as a witness. The legal issue of whether such evidence was admissible to show Winters' identity, motive, and intent in the murder case was a close question. Clarence Darrow would argue strenuously in the appeal that such evidence should not have been admitted.

The answer to the question, "how much evidence does the State have?" depended, in part, on how truthful Winters was with his attorneys. Tupper waived his opening argument—a sign that he recognized that surprises might come from Winters as well as from Trainor.

It is not only evidence that can sway a jury. Jurors pay less attention to a court's legalistic reasonable doubt instruction when a defendant is charged with the brutal murder of a vulnerable victim. Raymond Trainor was not going to rely on circumstantial evidence. The special prosecutor intended to convict John Winters by showing them what a murderer had done to Cecelia Gullivan.

⇒ 10 ⇐
Exhibit 35

THE INITIAL TESTIMONY of Assistant Director of the State Laboratory Dr. Fred Kent, who performed the autopsy on Cecelia Gullivan, "was of a colorless character" according to a *Boston Globe* reporter who had covered so many murders that even the most appalling wounds were of little interest.[1]

Special Prosecutor Raymond Trainor's next question to Dr. Kent got the jaundiced crime reporter's attention:

> Q. (Trainor): At the time you performed the autopsy on Miss Gullivan did you take some part of her body away with you?
> A. (Dr. Kent): Yes sir.
> Q. What did you take?
> A. I took the head.
> Q. And have you Miss Gullivan's head?
> A. I have.
> Q. Have you it here in court ready to produce?
> A. Yes.[2]

Jurors, reporters, and spectators—aghast or fascinated or both—awaited Dr. Kent's production of the head. Trainor had something else in mind. Rumors that Frank Cone had been having an affair with Cecelia Gullivan continued to swirl in Windsor. There were anonymous suggestions that the murdered woman was pregnant. The innuendo had perhaps reached jurors.

The special prosecutor asked the medical examiner about something the autopsy revealed:

> Q. (Trainor): What did you discover upon further examination of the body?
> A. (Dr. Kent): A large fibrous tumor in the uterus.

Exhibit 35

Q. How large was it?

A. It was approximately one and a half times as large as a fair-sized grapefruit.

Q. Was this girl pregnant?

A. She was not.

Q. Could a man have sexual intercourse with this woman?

A. It didn't seem possible.

Q. The vagina—how much entrance, with that tumor blocking, could there be?

A. On my examination, up to the second joint of the forefinger.

Raymond Trainor had simultaneously eliminated a motive for Frank Cone and suggested what might trigger a rapist's rage. The prosecutor knew how to keep the specter of a severed head in the minds of jurors: "That is all we have at present from the Doctor," said Trainor.

It was 4:25 p.m. Friday afternoon and court was adjourned.

"State to Exhibit Head of Miss Gullivan" read the front page of Saturday's *Boston Globe*, reporting a "crowded courtroom shocked into rapt attention."[3] "Shock" was apt because no jury in the history of Vermont criminal law had ever heard a prosecutor offer to introduce such gruesome evidence.

The extraordinary prosecutorial decision to offer the murder victim's head as evidence demonstrated at least one indisputable fact: Raymond Trainor was determined to convict John Winters for Cecelia Gullivan's murder irrespective of the fairness of the trial.[4]

The expectation that Trainor would recall Dr. Kent to the stand to exhibit the head had one predictable result: spectators clamored to get into the Woodstock courthouse. Hundreds stood in line on a cold Saturday morning in January awaiting the resumption of the medical examiner's testimony. Long tables were placed in the courtroom to accommodate reporters. Many were from "large metropolitan dailies" noted the *Bethel Courier* with misplaced pride.[5]

Although the special prosecutor would also have the director of the state laboratory, Dr. Charles Whitney, testify, it was the junior Dr. Kent that Trainor prompted to "fit the weapons" found in Winters' home into Cecelia Gullivan's head wounds.

Trainor was concerned enough about the qualifications of his witness to intentionally solicit a misleading answer from Dr. Kent:

Q. (Trainor): Have you performed autopsies?

A. (Dr. Kent): I have, sir.

Q. In murder cases?
A. Yes sir.
Q. How many?
A. Approximately 125–150.

As Trainor well knew, less than two dozen of Dr. Kent's autopsies were murder cases.[6] But a prosecutor who is about to ask his medical examiner to demonstrate autopsy findings by showing jurors the head of the murder victim must do all he can to make him credible.

If the packed courtroom's anticipation of a severed head was high, so was the palpable discomfort of the judge and attorneys now that the specter was before them. Even Trainor faltered after initially asking Dr. Kent if he could demonstrate the nature of the wounds "using the head."

The usually unflappable special prosecutor added, "Can you cover it with a sheet or something?" Dr. Kent asked for bath towels. Trainor, regaining his composure, asked, "You now have the head, wrapped in towels, that was taken from the body of Miss Cecelia Gullivan? And that is State's exhibit 35?"

When his witness answered affirmatively, the prosecutor moved to introduce the head as evidence: "For the purpose of this demonstration we offer this as an exhibit." Then—in perhaps the single most stunning sentence in the trial transcript—Judge Thompson declared, "There is no objection, and it may be received as an exhibit."

The failure of the defense to object to an exhibit so prejudicial to the defendant and such obvious grounds for reversal was inexplicable. It is conceivable that attorneys Herbert Tupper and Fred Bicknell believed that they would be able to make their own use of Exhibit 35. The startlingly inept cross-examination of Dr. Kent by Bicknell suggests he thought he could undermine the medical examiner's testimony by demonstrating that a chisel and spring could not have caused Cecelia Gullivan's fatal wounds.

Clarence Darrow almost certainly asked the attorneys why they had not preserved, among all their other exceptions, the strongest argument for overturning the conviction. Whatever the reason, they did not.

The defense attorneys had, in fact, made almost no objection to the myriad exhibits Trainor had introduced in his quest for little links in the chain of circumstantial evidence. Now, as the prosecutor had done for each of the previous thirty-four exhibits, he indicated to the court that he would attach an exhibit tag. Judge Thompson had his own objection: "It is not necessary to attach the tag."

Exhibit 35

Spectators strained to see, but the attorneys from both sides stood in such a way as to shield the ghoulish view. Dr. Kent held Cecelia Gullivan's head on his knee as he began his testimony. One man ran from the courtroom, but no women did. John Winters sat "placidly chewing gum . . . with his face utterly devoid of expression."[7]

Two instruments taken from Winters' house more than a week after the murder had been introduced into evidence. Exhibit 23 was a chisel beveled on one side and smooth on the other; exhibit 24, a steel spring. "Murder weapons!" Trainor had exclaimed in his opening argument without identifying either beyond claiming that Cecelia Gullivan's head wounds "could" have been caused by the chisel and the spring.

Now, the prosecutor and his expert sought to remove any doubt with a demonstration unprecedented in Vermont criminal jury history. "Dr. Kent, if you will step down here facing the jury, with exhibit 35," requested the prosecutor. The young medical examiner did so, speaking matter-of-factly to the jurors: "This is the right side of the head toward you gentlemen."

For the next hour, Dr. Kent meticulously inserted exhibits 23 and 24 into exhibit 35. Turning Cecelia Gullivan's head this way and that, the medical examiner explained his autopsy findings as he demonstrated the "fit" of the instruments to the terrible wounds.

The spring had caused a hole in the cheekbone that Dr. Kent initially thought was a bullet hole. The several blows to the skull—some of which cut the hair and scalp clean off—were consistent with cuts that could have been made by a chisel. Where the instruments did not quite fit the wound size, the prosecutor made sure the State's expert had an answer:

> Q. (Trainor): The wound would be a little shrunk?
> A. (Dr. Kent): Yes, this specimen is in a formaldehyde preservative and has, of course, a tendency to shrink.
> Q. You have fitted this chisel into all the wounds on the side and top of the head?
> A. Yes sir.

When Special Prosecutor Trainor turned to defense attorney Fred Bicknell and said, "Your witness," there was only one good question a lawyer (knowing the answer) could ask on cross-examination. Bicknell asked it:

> Q. Dr. Kent, did you find blood on either the spring or the chisel?

A. I did not find blood on either.

Unfortunately for John Winters, that question was preceded by a disastrous attempt by his attorney to cast doubt on Dr. Kent's findings about the angle of the blows struck by the murderer. When the defense attorney sought to demonstrate his theory with the chisel, Judge Thompson interjected, "You are holding it exactly opposite from the way Dr. Kent held it."

Far worse was the length of the cross-examination. With Cecelia Gullivan's head visible to the jurors, defense attorney Bicknell questioned Dr. Kent about Miss Gullivan's position in the bed when the first blows were struck.

> Q. (Bicknell): Did your investigation of the wounds lead you to believe she sat up?
> A. (Dr. Kent): Yes, I think she did.
> Q. What was there that made you think she sat up?
> A. The wounds on the side of the head and the wounds on the side of the face.

Defense attorney Bicknell had now created a visual of a terrified victim for a jury already aghast at the sight of her head. Then he made it worse:

> Q. During the time she was sitting up do you believe she was conscious?
> A. I believe she was conscious when she received the first blow.

The prosecutor knew how to exploit an advantage when the defense gave him one. On redirect, Trainor asked:

> Q. Dr. Kent, do you have an opinion as to the time it took her to die after the injuries inflicted on her head and face?
> A. It might have taken one or two hours.

Judge Thompson could read the faces of the shocked jury. He asked the only question that could give the jury some respite: "In your opinion, Doctor, was Miss Gullivan conscious after these injuries were inflicted?" Even the junior Dr. Kent, who sat comfortably with Cecelia Gullivan's head on his knee, realized that his answer had to be "No sir."

Exhibit 35

The jury, although composed of many jurors familiar with the blood and butchery common to farm life, could not be expected to remain dispassionate. "Presumption of innocence" is merely an abstraction when jurors have before them the defendant and the mutilated head of the murder victim.

The Link in the Chain

"THE STATE WILL SHOW YOU little links in the long chain of circumstantial evidence that point conclusively to but one man," Special Prosecutor Raymond Trainor asserted in his opening argument. But the strength of the chain was entirely dependent on one link: connecting John Winters to the break-in and assault at the Evarts house on the same night as the murder of Cecelia Gullivan.

After the shocking introduction of the head, the prosecution again used demonstrative evidence that, if nothing else, emphasized to jurors the murderous invasion of the victim's home. Sheriff Wallis Fairbanks recreated Cecelia Gullivan's bedroom, displaying before the jury the bed, mattress, sheets, and quilt. Defense objections that the recreation was inaccurate and prejudicial were rejected by the court.

Judge Frank Thompson overruled objections to the State's evidence so often in the first few days of trial that the defense lawyers' response, "May we have an exception to the ruling of the Court?" was a common refrain. By taking an "exception," the defense preserved the right to argue to the Vermont Supreme Court that the ruling by Judge Thompson was reversible error.

Raymond Trainor knew how to make the most of an advantage when a court gave him one. Confident that Judge Thompson would allow nearly limitless reign to the State, the special prosecutor pressed to introduce prejudicial evidence. He calculated that the defense would then have to put Winters on the stand to rebut it. Trainor had no doubt about the result if he could cross-examine John Winters.

Trainor called Winters' co-worker at Cone, George Putnam, as a witness. Putnam told the jury how the two men had spent early Saturday evening of November 6 together. They had made various stops to obtain illicit liquor and gone to the train station looking for Putnam's woman friend.

Putnam testified that while awaiting the train, Winters had crossed the street to speak to Stephanie Cole, who was standing in front of her store. He returned to tell Putnam that "I told her I had twenty dollars to spend if she wanted a good time and she said that wasn't enough."

The special prosecutor then asked a question to which he surely knew the answer given his meticulous trial preparation: "What else were you and he talking about?" Putnam replied, "John said you know I served time up on the hill. I didn't serve as much as I was supposed to. I would not have served that except the girl's father . . . "[1]

Defense attorney Herbert Tupper, his voice rising as he did, interrupted. "Just a moment . . . how is that material?" Judge Thompson replied, "I think we will leave the answer as is." Tupper asked for an exception. But now the jury knew that John Winters had served time in Windsor State Prison for sexual assault.

The prejudicial testimony that the defendant was an ex-convict accomplished the special prosecutor's objective of persuading the jury that Winters could commit crimes, but Trainor was not any closer to linking him to the murder of Cecelia Gullivan. The strength of the link depended entirely on one witness—and on whether Judge Thompson would allow her testimony.

Trainor wasted little time in putting the link to the test. In calling Bessie Pandjiris to the stand, he quickly established that she was a live-in nurse for Miss Margaret Evarts at 7 North Main Street. When Trainor asked, "Were you at 7 North Main Street on November 7, 1926?" defense attorney Tupper interjected: "We fail to see the connection of this line of testimony to the defendant. I would like to have the State make a more specific offer."

Special Prosecutor Trainor responded, "We are perfectly willing to do so. The evidence will show that this defendant grabbed this woman, and struck her, and dragged her to the floor and gouged her eyes, put his thumb in her mouth and his hand in her vagina, and asked her if she would take it."

Judge Thompson said, "We will receive the evidence." One can almost hear the desperation in defense lawyer Tupper's voice: "This, is undoubtedly, the most important legal question that will arise in this trial. May I have a general exception without having to object to every question?" The fate of John Winters would now depend on whether his attorneys could shake the nurse's identification of the Evarts house intruder.

When Judge Thompson ruled that the State could introduce the Evarts evidence, the experienced Trainor had already set the stage. The

State had dismissed its earlier charge that Winters had broken in "with intent to rob." It did not fit the prosecutor's narrative.

The special prosecutor prepared his witness well. The prosecution's theory that the murder was not committed by a robber was supported by the fact that money and jewelry in plain sight in Gullivan's bungalow was not taken. Trainor needed to persuade the jury that the Evarts house intruder was not a robber either.

Bessie Pandjiris testified that the man who assaulted her pushed her night dress "well up over my body. He put his thumb in my mouth, and I bit it. He made a vaginal insertion with his hand. He said, 'do you want it?'" Trainor asked, "Who was the man that assaulted you?" His witness answered, "John Winters."

Herbert Tupper was a much more skilled cross-examiner than his co-counsel Fred Bicknell. But try as he might, he could not diminish the formidable Mrs. Pandjiris' identification. "Didn't you say that the police 'called to ask me if it couldn't be John Winters, and I said no, and they told me not to make up my mind too quickly?'" asked Tupper. "No, I have never said that" replied the State's witness.

Tupper kept at it:

> Q. (Tupper): Were you asked on Sunday morning after the assault by anyone if you knew who the man was?
> A. (Pandjiris): I don't recall that question.
> Q. Do you remember saying to anyone at that time you did not know who the man was?
> A. No, that is not the impression I had.
> Q. Didn't you say to reporters that you had no idea who your assailant was?
> A. No I don't think I said that.

But if Tupper was making any headway with the jury, all was lost when he asked, "Isn't it true that you said, 'It does not seem possible that it was John Winters?'" When Pandjiris answered "Yes, but . . . " the defense attorney was quick enough to prevent her from finishing the sentence.

But his quickness was no match for the special prosecutor, who knew that with a sympathetic judge, he could ask Bessie another question: "When you said you didn't see how your assailant could have been Winters, you started to explain—will you now?" "Yes," replied the nurse, "it came to my mind all that Tottie had done for John Winters and other members of his family, and he knew that she was helpless, and it didn't seem possible that he would come to her house to hurt her." That reply was what jurors remembered about the cross-examination.

Bessie Pandjiris' response gave Trainor the opening to ask on redirect examination if Miss Tottie's physical condition would allow her to testify. When the nurse replied, "No, she has failed ever since this happened," Judge Thompson readily agreed that Miss Evarts was too infirm to be a witness. If Tottie was less certain than Bessie Pandjiris that the intruder was John Winters, jurors would never know.

All that remained of significance in the State's case was the identification of burrs found by Miss Tottie's housekeeper on and near Bessie Pandjiris where none had been before. The burrs found on Cecelia Gullivan's sleeping porch had already been introduced into evidence. And so too had the burrs from John Winters' trousers. It was more than "a little link" in the circumstantial evidence chain.

Special Prosecutor Trainor now redirected the jury' attention to the early evening of Saturday, November 6. During the death cell interrogation, Detective E. A. Brown had asked Winters if he was in the pool room beneath the Victory Cafe at 9 p.m. on Saturday evening, November 6. Winters said "no." Trainor then called Frank Russell to the stand.

Q. (Trainor): Do you know John Winters?
A. (Russell): Yes sir.
Q. Did you see him on Saturday night, November 6?
A. Yes sir.
Q. Where?
A. In the pool room under the Victory Cafe.
Q. What time?
A. Very near nine o'clock.
Q. What was he doing?
A. Nothing, just sitting there.
Q. Did a lady come in there?
A. Yes.
A. Who?
A. Miss Gullivan.
Q. How long had you known her?
A. Practically all my life, I guess.
Q. Is another business conducted in the same room as the pool room?
A. Shoeshine and Shoe Repair.

Q. Is there any obstruction between the pool room and the shoe stand?

A. No.

Q. How far was John Winters from Miss Gullivan?

A. Probably 9 or 10 feet.

Q. Was she facing him?

A. No sir.

Q. Did you watch Winters?

A. Yes.

Q. What did you notice?

A. He kept his eyes on her and watched her all the time she was in there.

Q. How long?

A. Probably about three minutes as long as it took for her to get her shoes.

Q. Anything more than that?

A. No, he just watched her.

⇒ 12 ⇐

The Defense

JUDGE FRANK THOMPSON'S DENIAL of the defense motion to strike the Evarts house evidence eliminated any plan Winters' lawyers might have had for keeping him off the witness stand. A defendant cannot be compelled to testify in his own defense, but Special Prosecutor Raymond Trainor made it almost compulsory by presenting a case overwhelming in evidence and emotion.

There could be no counter to the impact of the prosecution's unprecedented use of the victim's head as an exhibit, but defense attorneys began with the only hope they had for appealing to juror sympathy. Just before the defense put on its first witness, John Winters' wife entered the courtroom with the couple's newborn in her arms. It was the first time he saw his new son.

But whatever the effect the tableau of the defendant's wife, baby, mother, and aunt may have had on jurors, it did not create a reasonable doubt of Winters' guilt. That could only come through the testimony of defense witnesses and the defendant if he chose to testify.

Winters' lawyers called several witnesses to the stand including Winters' in-laws, uncle, sister, and mother, Maggie Winters. None had helpful evidence. Maggie testified that John had dropped off one of his little boys at her apartment early Saturday evening. She next saw her son Sunday morning: "It looked like he had been drinking the night before."[1] Trainor did not cross-examine.

Defense Attorney Herbert Tupper then attempted to raise suspicion about Frank Cone. The prosecution's concern that the defense might attempt to divert the jury by raising questions about Cone's credibility was well-founded. "Just what do you want to know?" Cone testily responded to Tupper's question about what streets the married Cone had taken to and from Gullivan's house. "I wouldn't attempt to tell you," Cone replied when pressed again.

Special Prosecutor Trainor had carefully orchestrated Frank Cone's testimony to emphasize three points: Cone went to Gullivan's home at 10:00 p.m. on Saturday night only to discuss business; at Cecelia's suggestion they had taken a drive without stopping; and Cone was in his own home by 11:30 p.m., having dropped Cecelia at her house no later than 11:15 p.m.

Defense attorney Tupper knew that jurors would have difficulty believing that a married man went to an attractive woman's home at 10:00 p.m. on a Saturday night only to talk business. Was Cone telling the truth about the drive and the time he got home? The defense called as a witness George Cook, an employee of Cone Automatic. Cook testified that he knew Cone and Cecelia Gullivan.

Tupper asked his witness if he recognized Frank Cone's Hudson automobile. Trainor objected to the question as "immaterial." The defense attorney responded, "I offer to show this witness saw Mr. Cone and Miss Gullivan parked beside the road sometime after 11:00 p.m. Saturday, November 6."

Judge Thompson asked, "What do you claim for that?" Tupper said, "I don't claim anything for it, except that it was a period of time later than Mr. Cone has testified about." "It is excluded, and you may have an exception," ruled Thompson.

There was now only one witness who could persuade the jury that there was insufficient evidence to prove beyond a reasonable doubt that John Winters murdered Cecelia Gullivan.

On the afternoon of February 9, 1927, three months after he was first taken into custody on the suspicion of murder, John Winters took the stand in his own defense. He responded to attorney Fred Bicknell's first question in a clear and confident voice. The defendant was the only person who knew the truth of his answer:

Q. Did you kill Cecelia Gullivan?
A. No sir.

The defense lawyer's challenge was to ask follow-up questions that could make the denial credible. Bicknell led Winters through a narrative that up until midnight of November 6 varied little from the prosecution's story. But the difficulty for the defense was that the jury was awaiting an answer to the question the prosecution had posed: Where was Winters in the early hours of November 7?

Without the Evarts evidence to contradict it, Winters' story of a postmidnight odyssey from closed dance hall, to stumbling down a hill looking for water, and then to an abandoned farm to steal apples may have had the ring of plausibility—if any juror had experienced inebriated wanderings. At the very least, the defense would have had an account that the State could not disprove.

But confronted with Bessie Pandjiris' identification of Winters as her assaulter, the defense attorney's only option on direct examination was to plant seeds of reasonable doubt in the minds of the jurors.

Winters' injured thumb was visible to a jury that had listened to the nurse testify she bit the thumb of her assailant. Bicknell asked the defendant to step off the stand and show it to the jury. In response to his lawyer's question, "When did you first notice you hurt it?" Winters responded, "Sunday morning." That could not have been helpful.

Bicknell attempted to offer innocent explanations for three incriminating aspects of the trousers Winters wore that night: the tear, the burrs, and the blood. Winters testified that the tear and the burrs must have come when he stumbled down the hill in a search for water or when he attempted to steal apples.

The defense attorney believed there was a better explanation for the blood. The previous April, Winters had cut off his finger while working at his house. Special Prosecutor Trainor objected that Bicknell's questions were immaterial.

"It is for this purpose," asserted the defense attorney to the court. "We offer to show that at the time he cut off his finger he was wearing the trousers that are in this case." Judge Thompson asked, "Do you offer to show he got blood on his trousers at that time?" Bicknell responded, "No we can't; we can show his opportunity to have done it." "Excluded," ruled the judge. "You may have an exception."

Before completing his direct examination, Bicknell asked Winters a curious question: "Did Mr. Trainor and Detective Brown tell you something about a doctor?" "Yes," Winters responded.

Q. (Bicknell): Do you remember the name of that Doctor?
A. (Winters): Dr. Heidel, I believe.
Q. Was it Dr. Jekel?
A. Yes, that was it.
Q. Who told you about Dr. Jekel?
A. Mr. Trainor.
Q. What did he tell you?
A. He told me that this man drank something and went crazy and done things that he didn't know he was doing.

In the State's five-day death cell interrogation of Winters, the "Dr. Jekel" story may have been just another prosecutorial ploy to prompt an admission of guilt. Or it may have been prosecutor Trainor's last attempt to provide Winters with an avenue that could save him from the electric chair. Whatever the prosecutor's motive, Trainor now knew that Winters' attorneys were not arguing that their client was incapable of forming the intent to commit murder because of insanity or intoxication.

"Winters in Composed Manner Denies Killing Miss Gullivan," reported the *Rutland Herald*, noting his "clear and decisive voice without a trace of nervousness."[2] That was about to change.

When Raymond Trainor rose to question John Winters, the forty-nine-year-old Irish American prosecutor confronting the thirty-two-year-old Irish American defendant knew something about "tough nuts": cross-examination is a good place to crack them.

Trainor had another advantage. Winters had been questioned so often during the five-day death cell interrogation that his answers were often contradictory. Windsor County State's Attorney Robert Twitchell had extensively questioned Winters in the first two days of interrogation. Trainor and Winters had at least this in common—both thought the state's attorney was inept.

The special prosecutor had to reopen questioning of witnesses that Twitchell had handled. Winters was often misled by Twitchell's confusing questions. Trainor asked Winters if he had ever lied to Twitchell during the interrogation. "After Tuesday [the second day in the interrogation] I did," responded Winters.

The prosecutor pressed the defendant:

Q. (Trainor): Every time you said anything?
A. (Winters): Well, practically anything, yes.
Q. Some of the things you told him were the truth weren't they, John?
A. Some.
Q. And some were lies?
A. Yes.

The prosecutor quickly pivoted to a question he knew Winters would have to answer truthfully:

Q. Are you the John Winters who pleaded guilty to the charge of rape in this court room in January 2013?

A. I am.

But the most devastating sequence of the cross-examination came when Winters surprised Trainor with an answer:

Q. Did you talk with Mrs. Cole when you and Putnam went to the railroad station on Saturday, November 6 at about 8 o'clock?
A. I did not.

The astonished prosecutor asked:

Q. You had no talk with her at all Saturday night?
A. None whatsoever.
Q. You didn't then go back to Putnam and tell him that you offered her $20 if she would go out with you for a good time?
A. No.
Q. You are positive about that?
A. Positive.

Any benefit of doubt jurors might afford Winters for responses coerced in a death cell interrogation evaporated when they heard an answer that directly contradicted the testimony of Putnam and Mrs. Cole, neither of whom had reason to lie.

Special Prosecutor Trainor saw the crack he had been looking for:

Q. You lied when you said you were not in the pool room on the night of November 6.
A. Yes.
Q. Why did you lie?
A. Because Detective Brown said he had a handful of my hair.
Q. Did you believe him?
A. Yes.

Trainor would claim in his closing argument that this answer was tantamount to a confession. Whatever it was, there was very little chance that jurors found Winters' next answers credible:

Q. Did you see Miss Gullivan in that pool room Saturday night?
A. I did not.
Q. Are you sure?

A. Absolutely.

The confidence of John Winters began to wane in the vise of Raymond Trainor's relentless cross-examination. As contradiction followed contradiction, the defendant's answers became less certain.

"Yes" was the defendant's response when the prosecutor asked if he remembered what he did up until midnight of November 6. "What about after midnight?" asked the special prosecutor. "Things is hazy" replied Winters.

Winters' explanations for his torn trousers and the burrs and blood on them came easily the day before when his own attorney was leading him. But the courtroom was Raymond Trainor's arena now. The special prosecutor finished his cross-examination with three questions that John Winters could no longer confidently answer:

> Q. You don't know where you got that tear in your trousers, do you?
> A. No.
> Q. And you don't know where you got the burrs on your clothes?
> A. No.
> Q. And you don't know where you got the blood?
> A. No.

Confronted with a cross-examination that devasted the credibility of his client, the defense attorney sought to minimize the significance of Winters' rape conviction. Bicknell claimed that the conviction secured by then Windsor County State's Attorney Trainor from the eighteen-year-old defendant was for statutory rape—not forcible rape.

"That is not true," retorted Trainor. Judge Thompson cautioned Bicknell: "If you open the issue, the court will allow the State to respond as fully as it wishes." The defense lawyer chose not to take the risk.

Special Prosecutor Trainor saved Detective E. A. Brown for the State's rebuttal. The attorney general's prosecutor and the attorney general's investigator had exquisitely choreographed the final act of the State's case.

Was Winters ever coerced during the five-day death cell interrogation? Was he ever told he could not have a lawyer? Did he ever deny that he was in Tottie Evarts' house on November 7 or that he killed Miss Gullivan? "No" answered Detective Brown to each question.

"Did you ever tell John Winters that you found hair in the hand of Cecelia Gullivan?" asked the prosecutor. "I did," replied Detective Brown.

"Did you tell him the truth when you said that?" asked Trainor. "I did," responded Brown. The question and answer were orchestrated.

Trainor did not ask whether—as Winters claimed—Brown had told him that Winters' hair was found in the victim's hand. The hair in Cecelia Gullivan's hand was her own. How much of the detective's testimony was balanced between truth and lie was known only to Trainor, Brown, and John Winters.

But Winters' attorneys did know this: the attorney general's prosecutor and investigator believed the ends justified the means in the prosecution of the defendant for the murder of Cecelia Gullivan. At this point of the trial, the jurors almost certainly did as well.

The defense did not cross-examine Detective Brown.

⇒ 13 ⇐

The Verdict

O<small>N</small> F<small>EBRUARY</small> 16, 1927, one month after prospective jurors had been summoned to the Woodstock courthouse, Attorney General J. Ward Carver stood before the jury. The attorney general had not examined or cross-examined a single witness in *State v Winters*. He knew that the most significant portion of the State's closing—its rebuttal after the defense arguments—would be done by Special Prosecutor Raymond Trainor.

Attorney General Carver also knew what every attorney general who runs for election knows: the more sensational the case, the greater the publicity. Trainor had teed up the ball. Carver did not intend to miss it.

"John Winters wanted to raise hell. That's what John Winters wanted. Were there two men in Windsor covered with burrs assaulting defenseless women?" exhorted the attorney general, his voice rising as he did so.[1] His argument was more beneficial to his political well-being than to a jury. Defense attorneys Herbert Tupper and Fred Bicknell needed only to persuade one juror that the State's case was flawed.

Tupper began the defense closing argument by challenging the "inquisitorial tactics" of the State. It was no wonder, he argued, that Winters made inconsistent statements during a five-day death cell interrogation that was intended to break him. Nor, contended the defense attorney, was it any wonder that Bessie Pandjiris identified Winters when Detective E. A. Brown brought the defendant to the Evarts house and reenacted the assault scene.

Attorney Bicknell continued the defense's challenge. He emphasized questions that must have occurred to jurors as well. Why did Winters carry a chisel and steel spring to the murder scene? Why would the murderer have taken the cellar window and thrown it in Mill Pond? "Evidence Is Circumstantial Says Bicknell in Strong Argument for Defense," headlined the *Rutland Herald*.[2]

When Raymond Trainor rose to give the State's rebuttal argument, he didn't begin with evidence. He began with John Winters. This man is a coward, declared the prosecutor. If Winters thought himself a tough nut, it was as personal a remark as Special Prosecutor Trainor could make in a court of law.

Trainor's summation again demonstrated his mastery of stretching the bounds of appropriate argument and instinct for compelling narrative. As he had done in his opening, Trainor claimed that the defense was unable to disprove the chain of circumstantial evidence—though the obligation was on the State to prove, not the defendant to disprove.

Raymond Trainor reserved for his final argument an answer to questions raised by the defense. "Burglar's tools!" asserted the special prosecutor—that was the reason Winters had carried a chisel and spring. "What in heaven's name would he take: a toothbrush and can of baking powder?"

And now the prosecutor had one last opportunity to remind the jurors of Winters' criminal record. "Nobody but a criminal would take a cellar window from a house. The man who did that was a post-graduate in fingerprints. For six years John Winters had heard all about fingerprints. He took the window to the float and washed away those tell-tale marks."

"We have been here a month to find out who was the murderer of this wonderful woman. It is your duty to safeguard women from criminals of the type who killed Miss Gullivan." Trainor's dramatic summation "clearly showed its effects on jurors as well as on spectators who filled the courtroom."[3]

The State had persuaded the jury beyond a reasonable doubt that the murderer of Cecelia Gullivan was someone *like* John Winters. But had it proved beyond a reasonable doubt that it *was* John Winters?

The morning of Friday, February 18, 1927, was another cold winter's day in a stretch that must have seemed interminable to a jury whose duty began a month before. The trial had been interrupted four times—twice by jurors' illness, once by the death of a juror's father, and once when the court stenographer was snowbound. One day of the trial, the temperature was 31 degrees below zero. The wooden benches in the Woodstock courtroom were never warm.

Judge Frank Thompson's instructions to the jury included charges of first-degree and second-degree murder. (The death penalty could only be imposed upon a defendant convicted of first-degree murder.) As jurors listened to a circumstantial evidence instruction far more favorable to the State than to the defendant, they were unanimous on two matters without discussion: each wished to begin deliberations that morning and none wished to spend the weekend reaching a verdict.

The jury received the case at 10:35 a.m. Of the twelve male jurors, the youngest was forty, the oldest seventy-one. An enterprising reporter calculated the average juror weight at over two hundred pounds, topped by 255-pound Hoyt Knight, the jury's foreman.[4] It was a jury that did not intend to skip a lunch paid for by the county even if they did reach a verdict by noon.

Shortly after 2:00 p.m. the jurors "paid the table girls their tips" and returned to the courthouse.[5] When at 2:30 p.m. the ringing of the courthouse bell signaled that the jury had a verdict, "throngs of people surged into the courtroom and occupied the stairs, hallways and corridors."[6]

John Winters was brought into court from the county jail, "his iron composure which has characterized him since the beginning of the trial completely gone."[7] The clerk of the court asked the defendant and the jurors to stand. Whether Winters "shook like a leaf" or "shuddered" or did neither, none could misread his tension nor the anxiety of his mother, sister, and aunt, Mrs. Laura Cooley, who sat behind him.

"Do you find the defendant, John C. Winters guilty?" the clerk asked the jury foreman. "We do," replied Hoyt Knight. "In what degree?" asked the clerk. "Guilty of murder in the first-degree," the foreman answered. "So say you all?" queried the clerk of the jury. "We do," the jurors said in unison.

When the clerk added "of murder in the first-degree?" jurors did not merely nod assent or answer yes, but instead "chorused 'guilty of murder in the first-degree.'"[8] The jury had reached its verdict before lunch. It was a testament to the extraordinary trial work of Special Prosecutor Raymond Trainor. Unless the conviction was reversed.

"Do you expect to take this case to the supreme court?" Judge Thompson asked defense attorney Herbert Tupper. His reply was brief and to the point: "Yes, your Honor."[9]

Sons

 HE EVENTS THAT BOUND Clarence Darrow to John Winters' fate spanned more than twenty years, from 1904 when Darrow's son Paul ran down five-year-old Harry Cooley, to 1927 when Winters' aunt asked the famous attorney to make good on his son's promise. But the connection of Laura Cooley to Clarence Darrow existed for only one reason: each was loyal to a son.

Shortly before Paul entered Dartmouth College, Darrow divorced Jessie Ohl, his wife of seventeen years. The forty-year-old Darrow's embrace of Chicago's social movement put him at the center of intellectual ferment that included a bohemian lifestyle. The charismatic Darrow attracted bright young women, "in a vast promiscuity carried on in his apartment," said his friend Edgar Lee Masters.[1]

Darrow's request for a divorce was no surprise to Jessie, for whom her husband was now "a man of the world." The couple separated as friends. "He was always generous . . . I could never say anything against him in the world," said Jessie. But Paul was not so forgiving. He told his father he never wanted to see him again.[2]

It was not a family dynamic likely to prompt a father to fulfill a secret pledge his son made as a college student more than twenty years before. But Clarence Darrow loved Paul deeply and always had. "My fear is that you and especially Paul may think I have done wrong," wrote Darrow to Paul's mother when they divorced. "I hope you know I love Paul and how miserable I should be if he did not love me . . . I have always cared for him more than anything on this earth."[3]

Shortly after graduation, Paul agreed to accompany his father on a trip west that included camping in the Canadian Rockies with his son's Dartmouth classmates. Paul's decision to accept his father's invitation to go on the trip may have been at the urging of his mother.

Darrow thought his son was far too subdued for a young man on a celebratory graduation trip. "Paul is very cautious. We could do more to make him enjoy himself," wrote Darrow to Jessie in July 1904—one month after their son kept the fatal accident a secret from both parents.[4]

Darrow had recently remarried, and he sent his former wife a new will leaving her and Paul two-thirds of his estate. Paul was to be the executor. "He likes books and so far, he has not shown any great liking for the law. He has a good business head, and I think he will get along all right," added his father.[5]

Darrow's assessment was accurate. A joint investment by father and son in a gas plant provided Paul with a career. In 1907 he moved to Colorado to manage the Greeley Gas Works. Paul had recently married a secretary from his father's law office, and they raised their three children in Colorado. Darrow frequently visited Greeley and became friends with many of his son's friends.[6]

"There is no joy like a child . . . Through the last thirty years nothing has brought me the consolation Paul has brought," Darrow wrote in 1915 to a friend who was expecting.[7] The Darrows' sale of Greeley Gas Works appeared to make them each financially secure. But father and son were investing in the soaring stock market.

Darrow wanted his son to move to Chicago to be closer to him. "Am not doing any law work except to take something easy once in a while without going to court . . . I read a good deal and loaf and do crossword puzzles . . . I am quite anxious for you to come here." Darrow's letter to Paul notified his son of the one exception he made to staying out of court: "I am to argue that case in Vermont [in] January."[8]

When Clarence Darrow learned that the consequence of fulfilling Paul's pledge would be to defend a death row inmate, he reacted as he always did. "Not only could I put myself in the other person's place, but I could not avoid doing so," said the "attorney for the damned."[9]

"The child is father to the man" was one of Clarence Darrow's most deeply held beliefs, embedded by decades of defending the damned. Much of society had modernized since the beginning of the twentieth century, but it would be decades before "domestic abuse" became a readily recognizable legal term. Yet it was as familiar to many households as the alcohol that often fueled it.

John Winters Sr. was a thirty-two-year-old hard-drinking itinerant quarryman working in West Rutland, Vermont. Twenty-two-year-old Margaret (Maggie) Cooley was living in Rutland, where she was largely responsible for raising her younger brothers Arthur and Henry. Whatever else Maggie's attraction to John Sr., part of it may have been the chance to be in her own household. John Winters Sr. and Maggie Cooley were married in Rutland in 1891. A son, John Cooley Winters, was born in 1894, followed two years later by daughter Anna.

As a boy, Paul Darrow kept a scrapbook of newspaper clippings about his father. John Winters could have kept one about *his* father, but it is doubtful that he did. John Winters Sr.'s name appeared periodically in the *Rutland Herald*: in 1895, a $5 fine for public intoxication; in 1904, when his son was nine, public intoxication (third offense); in 1905, jail for failing to pay $5 for public intoxication; in 1909, three months incarceration for repeated intoxication.[10] Fourteen-year-old John Winters may have left home by then.

Many had difficulty understanding why Mrs. Cooley—not a blood relative—could be so dedicated to the defense of John Winters. The explanation may have been directly related to the accident that killed five-year-old Harry Cooley. Laura Kendall married Maggie Winters' brother, Arthur Cooley, in 1897.

The twenty-five-year-old groom and his twenty-one-year-old bride soon established the stable family life that eluded the wife of John Winters Sr. Arthur had steady employment at Dartmouth College and the couple bought a house in Norwich just across the Connecticut River.

Their son was born there in 1899. Maggie Winters brought her children, John, then five, and Anna, then three, to see their new cousin Harry Cooley. Maggie Winters almost certainly preferred her children to be with their Uncle Arthur in Norwich than with their father John Sr. in Rutland.

When little Harry was killed, Arthur Cooley reached out to his sister Maggie to provide company to his distraught wife. The bond between a grieving mother who had just lost her only son and Maggie Winters' nine-year-old boy may well have been formed then.

Laura Cooley's devotion to John Winters was not a surprise to Clarence Darrow. Loyalty, said Darrow, was common in a family "who had seen [someone] in a different light from those who judged and hated and condemned [him] without trying to understand."[11]

"I will do all I can," Darrow wrote to his son. "I will see what I can do with an argument to the supreme court and if beaten will go to the governor."[12] Clarence Darrow knew how John Winters was raised long before he represented him. "The prisons are not filled with the children of parents who were too kind," wrote Darrow.[13]

His son had accidentally killed Mrs. Cooley's son. Clarence Darrow intended to do all he could to prevent the State of Vermont from deliberately killing the son of John Winters Sr.

⇒ 15 ⇐

Darrow and the Death Penalty

CLARENCE DARROW'S strident opposition to capital punishment was not "insane"—as one observer claimed—but its roots were dug deep in his childhood. Darrow's own fear of death may have stemmed from his father's work as an undertaker. "I remember the coffins piled in one corner of the shop, and I always stayed away from them as far as possible," he wrote in his autobiography.[1] But it was another memory of his father that planted the seeds of Darrow's lifelong crusade against the death penalty.

Amirus Darrow told his son of pushing his way to the front of boisterous spectators when, as a young man, he eagerly awaited the hilltop hanging of a murderer. When his father saw a black cap pulled over the man's head and a noose tightened around his neck, "he could stand no more." Darrow wrote that his father "felt ashamed for the rest of his life that he could have had that much of a hand in killing a fellow man."[2]

The story left an indelible mark on Darrow, who returned to it time and again in his speeches and debates about the wisdom of capital punishment. "They used to hang people on a high hill, so that everybody would be awed into goodness by the sight," Darrow sarcastically retorted to a prominent judge who claimed that the death penalty would deter crime.[3] "In the end this question is simply one of humane feelings against brutal feelings," he asserted.[4]

Darrow knew that the imposition of the death penalty was never as simplistic as weighing feelings. But he had a profound skepticism, born of a lifetime of advocacy, of the concept of justice. "Justice is something man knows little about. He may know something about charity and understanding and mercy, and he should cling to these as far as he can," said Darrow.[5] It was a clue to understanding how America's greatest trial lawyer might persuade the Vermont Supreme Court to reverse a conviction that would otherwise lead to the execution of John Winters.

It was a plea for mercy that prompted eight hundred Bennington residents—each of whom claimed to be supporters of the death penalty—to petition Governor Charles Bell in 1905 to grant clemency to Mary Rogers, who was sentenced to be hanged. Rogers had been convicted of murdering her husband for the insurance proceeds and enlisting the help of a farmhand who soon confessed to his role.

The Windsor County sheriff and the four deputies who were to hang Mary Rogers requested Governor Bell to excuse them from that duty. "If there are any who desire to retire from office, they are at liberty to do so," Bell replied.[6] The governor visited Rogers in her cell, where his professed "wish to save her" was secondary to his faithfulness to the death penalty.

Three-quarters of a century earlier, Governor Silas Jenison had a different view of what that faith should be. In his 1838 address to the legislature, Jenison called for abolition of capital punishment: "All experience shows that crime has not increased but diminished, as the criminal laws of a country have become less barbarous and vindictive."[7] The abolition bill passed the Vermont House but was defeated in the senate—a pattern that was repeated in subsequent attempts to eliminate the death penalty.

Governor Jenison was successful in persuading the legislature to end the practice of publicly executing convicted murderers. Henceforth, hangings were to take place within the yard of Windsor State Prison.[8] The legislature's acceptance of the governor's proposal may have been prompted by the public hanging of Archibald Bates in Bennington. Fifteen thousand spectators were at the execution, a turnout that a county fair would envy.[9]

Remarkably, there was no instance of capital punishment in Vermont for the next quarter century despite the retention of the death penalty. The absence was attributable to a process that afforded a convicted murderer the opportunity to petition the legislature for commutation of the sentence. In the five cases in which the death penalty would have been otherwise imposed, legislators commuted the sentences to life imprisonment.[10]

The explanation for the humane approach between 1838 and 1860 was due, in no small part, to Vermont governors and legislators having come of political age in "an era of idealism, optimism, and reform."[11] It was forcefully expressed by a select committee of the Vermont legislature on a bill to abolish punishment by death: "A boy who has a daily example [of crime] set before him . . . and now the State hangs him. For what? For being just what society made him."[12]

But that sentiment changed in the wake of the Civil War, an alteration that did not surprise Clarence Darrow. "In the presence of the wholesale slaughter of men the value of life is cheapened . . . followed in turn . . . by a large increase in . . . executions by the state," asserted Darrow.[13] It was a consequence he knew well in the decade following World War I.

On January 20, 1864, the yard of Windsor State Prison had far fewer spectators than had witnessed the public hanging of Archibald Bates in Bennington twenty-five years before. Governor Silas Jenison, whose proposal to abolish the death penalty came within three votes of passing, would not have found solace in the first implementation of the policy to hang murderers within prison walls instead of on public ways. That day, the State of Vermont hanged two men.

Vermont never again had multiple executions on one day, but between 1864 and 1905 ten men and one woman were hanged. The execution of Emeline Meaker in 1883 demonstrated, if nothing else, that application of capital punishment in Vermont was gender neutral. It was a useful precedent for Governor Bell, who needed it, when tens of thousands of pleas from all over America were added to the eight hundred Bennington residents who asked for mercy for Mary Rogers.

The difference between the relative obscurity of the hanging of Emeline Meaker and the literally international prominence of the Mary Rogers case was precipitated by the "yellow press" of the Hearst newspapers.[14] Her case became the first example of a Vermont murder sensationalized beyond the state's borders.

The ingredients newspapers were to mix so often in the next two decades to titillate the public were there: a brutal murder and prurient interest. Though Rogers may have been a plain woman with significant mental deficiency, reporters for the tabloid press tantalized their readers with lurid descriptions of a "murderess" who was a "voluptuous and good looking and much sought-after young woman with lustrous dark eyes and jet-black hair."[15]

Irrespective of the accuracy of the media's portrayal of Mary Rogers, Vermonters could not avoid the pending consequences of the application of Vermont's death penalty statute. It was not for lack of trying, at least among the many for whom her execution was unthinkable.

In 1904, with Mary Rogers confined to Windsor State Prison, sympathetic legislators introduced bills to abolish capital punishment and to commute her sentence. The initiative to end the death penalty failed in the house by a two-to-one margin—a not unexpected result. The greater surprise was the legislators' failure to commute the death sentence, as it had done at least a half-dozen times since the last hanging in 1891.[16]

The fifty-vote margin by which the motion for mercy was defeated was an indication that the Rogers case now stood as a marker for the death penalty. To favor commutation meant, especially for elected officials, that one opposed capital punishment. Governor Bell believed he knew his constituency best: "The people of Vermont think she should be hanged, and I am going to see that the sentence is carried out."[17]

Several attempts were made to prevent the governor from implementing his decision, including unsuccessful appeals to the Vermont Supreme Court and the United States Supreme Court.[18] Public appeals by prominent Vermonters for mercy were probably futile in the first instance, but such pleas had no chance in the wake of the Windsor State Prison scandal.

The allegations of corruption, misuse of prison labor, and other malfeasance that were to lead to the dismissal of the superintendent paled in comparison to the revelation that rumored sexual contact among inmates included frequent "visits" from a convicted rapist to the cell of Mary Rogers. Prison officials had an obvious motive in portraying the visits as consensual. Whether they were or not, her signed "admission" that she allowed access was even more reason an aroused public awaited execution day.[19]

When Mary Rogers was led to the scaffold on December 8, 1905, the forty witnesses selected to watch her hang were a fraction of those eager to know how a twenty-two-year-old female would confront her last moments. The influx of reporters prompted extra telegraphers to be added to ensure the nation would not have to wait to learn of Vermont's execution of a woman.

But wait they did, for at least an extra fourteen minutes. The stoicism of Mary Rogers as the black hood was placed over her head and the noose around her neck gave way to horror when the trap door opened. The new rope had not been measured for tension and the young woman's toes touched the earth. Deputies pulled frantically on the rope to lift her and held on as Rogers swung in the air for the quarter hour it took to strangle her to death.

The public outcry is easily imagined, as was the predictable attempt of prison officials to minimize the horrendous result. The superintendent denied that Rogers' feet had touched the ground and a statement by the three-member pool of reporters that witnessed the hanging was conveniently vague. But a deputy sheriff who was there said, "I had to turn my head away. May I never be commanded again to take part."[20]

It is difficult to imagine an execution that could do more to alter capital punishment in Vermont. But it took another "rope malfunction" to prompt the legislature to act. In 1912, Elroy Kent was the first to be sentenced to death since the gruesome ending of Mary Rogers. Again, the Windsor County sheriff's office brought the doomed prisoner to the scaffold. The rope was short enough to provide tension but not strong enough for the man's weight. Kent's neck was only partially broken, and he had to be hanged a second time.

"The spectacle . . . caused one to shudder in horror . . . Vermont [ought] to demand a change of statute."[21] Change came in 1913 when Vermont joined a dozen other states that replaced the gallows with the electric chair. The movement to supplant hanging with electrocution was premised on the belief that the latter was more humane, though legislators who favored efficiency could point to New York. It was the first state to use an electric chair (1890) and proficient enough to electrocute seven men in one day in 1912.[22]

By then, Clarence Darrow had already spent twenty-five years advocating for an end to capital punishment. In 1887, the thirty-year-old lawyer, newly arrived in Chicago, endorsed (and may have written) a statement of a group that "capital punishment is unnecessary [and] barbarous."[23]

Two years later, Darrow's voice was unmistakable. Speaking to Chicago's Sunset Club, he castigated its members for their silence when "a weak, ignorant boy of African descent . . . who had never known a kindly hand" was hanged in the city. "Strangled to death" said Darrow, by a society that "laid its hand upon this boy, but once."[24]

The decision to make Vermont's method of execution more "humane" included an appropriation for the installation of an electric chair in Windsor State Prison. Legislators debated the cost but not the penalty.[25] In 1916 the new instrument was placed in a "death chamber" adjoining the "death cell." Inmates, including twenty-one-year-old John Winters who was serving his sentence for rape, took notice.

Vermonters had to wait five years to determine the efficacy of the modern means of execution. In 1919, George Warner became the first man to die in Vermont's electric chair. Early on the morning of July 12, the condemned man was led fifteen steps from his death cell to the chamber, where he was strapped into the new device. A single shock of 2,000 volts—"a most successful operation," said the executioner—and Warner was pronounced dead three minutes later.[26]

A story long repeated in Windsor was that lights would dim throughout the town when the switch was thrown. Prison officials apparently shared that concern because the State electrocuted Warner at 3 a.m. when few homes had lights on. Even if apocryphal, there can be little doubt that inmates knew the instant their fellow inmate was executed.

As Darrow had foreseen, executions increased in the aftermath of World War I. Five states that had abolished the death penalty reinstated it. More than one hundred inmates were executed in the United States in 1920.[27] In a Roaring Twenties America that embraced capital punishment, Clarence Darrow often stood between life and death for a defendant.

"No client of mine had ever been put to death, and I felt that it would almost, if not quite kill me if it should ever happen," wrote America's most famous criminal defense lawyer.[28] In 1925, the sixty-seven-year-old Darrow's record was put to the ultimate test when he agreed to represent the brilliant, amoral, teenage sons of two of Chicago's wealthiest families. "Dickie" Loeb and Nathan Leopold had confessed to the kidnapping and brutal murder of fourteen-year-old Bobby Franks.

"The most cruel, cowardly, dastardly, murder in the history of American jurisprudence," claimed the Illinois state's attorney when the penalty phase of the case began. Assistant State's Attorney Joseph Savage argued to the judge that Darrow had his clients plead guilty because he was afraid to submit the case to a jury. Darrow's reply to the young prosecutor ("were you picked because of your name?") was characteristic: "We did plead guilty before your Honor because we were afraid."[29]

Darrow knew that jurors who heard the prosecution's evidence of the boy's brutal murder and the defendants' lack of remorse would not hesitate to recommend the death penalty. The only hope of saving the lives of Loeb and Leopold amid a frenzied public's demand for death was to persuade the sentencing judge that mercy meant more than justice. "Darrow Pleads for Mercy: Mobs Riot," proclaimed a Chicago newspaper.[30]

Darrow's genius as a defense attorney stemmed from an unerring sense of knowing what troubled a judge or jury—often before they themselves knew. He immediately pointed to a practice the judge recognized. "Coming into this courtroom with obscure defendants and saying to this court and prosecutor these boys ought not to be at large and willing to enter a plea of guilty and accept life imprisonment. How long do you think your Honor would hesitate? Do you suppose the State's Attorney would protest?"[31]

In the incredibly charged and exhaustively lengthy sentencing hearing, Darrow returned again to the hanging his father had witnessed— "hangings on a high hill, and the populace for miles around coming out to the scene." Those who knew Darrow best did not doubt his claim that he was "not pleading so much for these boys as I am for [those] to follow . . . who cannot be as well defended, those who may go down in the storm and tempest without aid."[32]

Darrow was now speaking to an audience far beyond the courtroom. "If these two boys die on the scaffold the details will be spread over the world. Every newspaper in America will carry a full account . . . Will it make men better or make men worse? . . . The question needs no answer. You can answer it from the human heart."[33]

When Darrow finished his plea, the courtroom was silent. On September 10, 1924, the court sentenced Loeb and Leopold to life imprisonment. Darrow told friends that he was looking forward to a retirement that would enable him to lead a campaign against capital punishment.[34]

Retirement had to wait. Two of his most famous trials, the Scopes monkey trial and the defense of Dr. Ossian Sweet, were ahead. Darrow publicly announced he was retiring from the practice of law on April 18, 1927, his seventieth birthday, to "devote himself to writing and speaking."[35] He would take no more cases.

One month later, as the newly retired Clarence Darrow completed his Dartmouth lecture, "Why I Am Against Capital Punishment," Laura Cooley handed him a letter.

1. Cecelia Gullivan in 1904. The twenty-one-year-old was a bridesmaid at her cousin's wedding. Courtesy of Christine Simonson, from the estate of Mary J. Schindler McMenamy.

2. Clarence Darrow and his son Paul, probably 1886 in Ashtabula, Ohio. Darrow was almost thirty and Paul was almost four. Darrow moved to Chicago in 1887.
Courtesy of Rare Books and Special Collections, University of Minnesota Law Library.

3. Twenty-one-year-old Paul Darrow was three days from his Dartmouth graduation on June 22, 1904. Findagrave.com.

4. Frank Cone founded the Cone Automatic Machine Company in 1916. The first person he hired was Cecelia Gullivan. Findagrave.com.

5. Workers in the Cone shop, circa 1920s. Workers, including the slender figure in the center, are not identified in the photo. Courtesy of Lee Baker.

6. Frank Cone in 1920. The "Roaring Twenties" were just starting.
Courtesy of the Springfield Art and Historical Society.

7. Front page of the *Boston Globe*, November 8, 1926.

8. Windsor State Prison. Vermont State Archives and Records Administration.

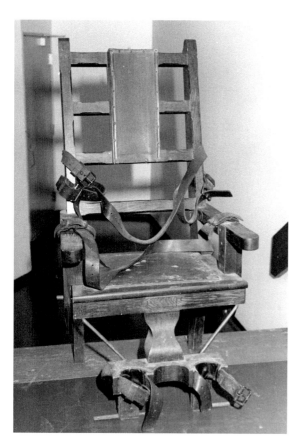

9. The legislature voted to replace the gallows with the electric chair in 1913 after botched hangings. In 1919, George Putnam became the first person to die in Vermont's electric chair. Vermont Historical Society.

10. John Winters. If his conviction for the
first-degree murder of Cecelia Gullivan was
upheld by the Vermont Supreme Court,
Winters would be the second person to die
in Vermont's electric chair.
Boston Globe, November 11, 1926.

14. Clarence Darrow preparing for reargument of *State v. Winters* before the
Vermont Supreme Court on March 8, 1929.
To the right of Darrow is co-counsel Herbert G. Tupper.
Courtesy of the Boston Public Library, Leslie Jones Collection.

15. The Vermont Supreme Court building. Less than a decade old when Darrow made his first appearance, the new courthouse was far more spacious than the supreme court's previous State House location. But it was not large enough to contain the hundreds of men and women who sought to get a glimpse of America's most famous lawyer. Photograph in Carol M. Highsmith's America Project in the Carol M. Highsmith Archive, Library of Congress.

18. Justices of the Vermont Supreme Court, 1928. From left to right: Sherman R. Moulton, George M. Powers, Chief Justice John H. Watson, Leighton P. Slack, Harrie B. Chase. Vermont State Curator's Office.

19. President Calvin Coolidge and Attorney General John Sargent. The
Vermonters were classmates at Ludlow's Black River Academy, where the older
and larger Sargent protected the younger and smaller Coolidge from hazing.
Wikimedia.

20. Harrie B. Chase. Wikimedia.

⇒ 16 ⇐

Exceptions

THE ASTONISHMENT OF Herbert Tupper and Fred Bicknell when they were told "a Mr. Darrow" wished to speak to them about the Winters case can be easily imagined. It must have struck them as particularly fortuitous that his offer of help came just as they were beginning to review the trial transcript and write the brief. But Clarence Darrow's reputation as an extraordinary lawyer came from his brilliance as a trial attorney, not as an author of appellate briefs.

Darrow could write well—he had even published two novels—but his great talent was oral argument. He cared little about "case law," the legal research that Tupper and Bicknell must do to support their written arguments. Darrow was not really interested in how the Vermont attorneys briefed the legal issues. He wanted to know when the case would be scheduled for oral argument.

The supreme court directed Winters' attorneys and the State's prosecutors to have all briefing completed before the commencement of the court's January 1928 term. Tupper told Darrow that he should expect *State v. Winters* to be heard as soon as the term opened. The Chicago lawyer could await the call, but the Vermont lawyers had to get to work.

Attorneys Tupper and Bicknell could not decide which "exceptions" (objections to Judge Frank Thompson's trial rulings preserved for appeal) to brief until a trial transcript was prepared. The diligent court stenographer, who had braved a snowstorm, typed the three-volume, 660-page trial record from her shorthand notes. There is not a single mistyped word in it. But Winters' lawyers believed it was replete with prejudicial errors by Judge Thompson.

The pencil markings against selected portions of the trial transcript demonstrate a careful search for excerpts that could support the defense lawyers' claim that Judge Thompson committed a reversible error. Tupper and Bicknell could, as well, see where their own failure to make timely objections to the court's rulings meant that they had failed to "preserve" for appeal issues of obvious error.

By far the most glaring omission was the defense attorneys' virtually inexplicable decision not to object to the special prosecutor's use of the victim's severed head as demonstrative evidence. If there had ever been a prosecutor in Vermont, or anywhere else in the United States, that had attempted such a thing, there is no record of a court allowing it.

There was nothing to be gained by lamenting their own mistakes. Tupper and Bicknell divided the review of the 660 pages between them. Both had busy private practices and other responsibilities too. One scrawled note inserted between the pages reads "don't forget to get sugar!" and another, "AT&T 143 5/8 Dupont 208."

Diligent as the lawyers were, it is virtually certain that on May 21, 1927, they were not thinking of work—nor were many others. Charles Lindbergh had touched down at Le Bourget airport outside of Paris, after his thirty-three-hour solo flight across the Atlantic Ocean. As he stepped from the *Spirit of St. Louis*, the twenty-five-year-old pilot was astonished by the frenzied multitude of 150,000 Parisians surrounding his airplane. Lindbergh was about to become the most famous man in the world.

Calvin Coolidge's enthusiasm for American aviation was matched by his distaste for celebrity. But in Lindbergh, he saw all that he valued in character: "modest, congenial, a man of good moral habits and regular in his business practices." President Coolidge sent a warship to bring Lindbergh back to the United States. "He has brought his unsullied fame home," the proud president declared to an enormous crowd gathered at the Washington Monument.[1]

To an observer of the Roaring Twenties, the explanation of the instantaneous ascent of Charles Lindbergh to godlike reverence was because "a disillusioned nation . . . spiritually starved on their recent newspaper diet of murder" craved a handsome, brave, and self-effacing hero.[2] But not quite yet.

Two weeks after Lindbergh's flight, the *Boston Globe*'s bold-print front-page headline "Darrow May Go to Winters' Aid" dwarfed a smaller front-page story about the hero's attempt to return to Paris from London: "Lindbergh Quits His Hop to Paris."[3] It was time for defense lawyers Tupper and Bicknell to get back to their brief.

A "brief"—the written argument submitted to the supreme court—seldom is. The filing by defense attorneys on behalf of John Winters was over twenty pages long. Written arguments filed with the Vermont Supreme Court must begin with a "Statement of the Case." The statement is the opportunity for lawyers to cast the evidence in a light as favorable as possible to their side. The defense had no favorable evidence.

The defense lawyers' statement of the case on behalf of John Winters implied, as they had unsuccessfully done at trial, that there was another suspect. "On Saturday evening, November 6th, shortly after 10 p.m., Miss Gullivan went to ride with Frank Cone . . . said Frank Cone left Miss Gullivan's home directly after their return. There was no direct testimony as to any other person seeing Miss Gullivan between that time and on Monday morning, November 8th [when] Frank Cone went to her bungalow and discovered her dead body."[4]

The implication that Cone could have been the murderer had no better chance of influencing the supreme court than it did the trial court. The challenge to the attorneys for the defendant was to craft a brief that could persuade the justices that one of the exceptions they made to Judge Thompson's rulings was sufficient to reverse the jury's murder verdict and grant John Winters a new trial.

Tupper and Bicknell decided to brief nine exceptions, any one of which they argued constituted reversible error. Two of the nine claimed prejudicial errors (objections to the State's closing argument and to the court's charge to the jury) were on the brief's last page and were never argued. Another two exceptions were objections to the testimony of medical examiner Dr. Fred Kent and Sheriff Wallis Fairbanks that marks on the victim's sheets and wall appeared to be foot marks.

Two more exceptions (an objection to the admission of testimony that Winters had offered Mrs. Stephanie Cole twenty dollars for a good time, and an objection to the recreation of the victim's sleeping porch in the courtroom) were not adequately briefed. The testimony of Mrs. Cole was characterized "as extremely prejudicial" but without citation to case law to support the assertion. The exception to the sleeping porch evidence cited cases but added, "they are not directly on point." It is seldom helpful to draw a court's attention to a weakness in your argument.

The cursory discussion of seven of the nine exceptions briefed by Tupper and Bicknell was indicative of the significance they attached to their two exceptions challenging the introduction of the Evarts house evidence. Seventeen pages of the twenty-three-page brief are devoted to strenuous legal argument that the trial court erred in allowing any testimony related to the break-in and assault.

"This is the most important issue in this trial," defense attorney Tupper had exclaimed to Judge Thompson when he objected to the court's decision to allow Special Prosecutor Raymond Trainor to introduce evidence of the break-in and assault at the Evarts house. Its significance was obvious to Clarence Darrow, who characterized it as "dangerous evidence . . . No [jury] could fail to be affected by it. Nothing could be more calculated to affect one."[5] The defense attorneys correctly asserted that as a general rule of law, evidence that the defendant committed another crime is not admissible in the trial for the crime charged. Bicknell and Tupper contended that application of the general rule to *State v. Winters* meant that it was reversible error for Judge Thompson to allow the jury to consider Evarts house evidence in the murder trial of John Winters—even if Winters was the man who broke into the Evarts house and assaulted Bessie Pandjiris.

As with all "general rules" of law, courts have identified circumstances where the rule does not apply. Evidence of another crime by the defendant may be admissible "to show a continuity of purpose" or "common scheme" or "motive" or "identity." The Vermont Supreme Court expected the State's brief to argue that evidence of Winters' acts at the Evarts house was admissible under any one or all the exceptions.

But the justices could not have imagined that the *defendant's brief* would admonish them not to lose sight of the exceptions. The brief was written by Fred Bicknell. He was no better at brief writing than at cross-examination. In contending that the general rule prohibiting the introduction of other crimes should keep out the Evarts house evidence, Bicknell repeatedly drew attention to circumstances where the general rule does *not* apply.

"The general rule is that proof that a person has been guilty of some other crime furnishes no evidence that he is guilty of the one for which he is being tried . . . But it does not follow that the Court erred in receiving the testimony . . . *There are certain well-established exceptions to the rule not to be lost sight of*"[6] (emphasis added). Bicknell then identified the exceptions.

With help like that from the defense lawyer, the State's brief, submitted by Windsor State's Attorney Robert Twitchell and Attorney General J. Ward Carver, devoted nearly all its pages to the gruesome facts of the case. Bicknell was as inept in arguing facts as he was the law. He dismissed Mrs. Pandjiris' graphic testimony of the assault with the assertion that "she was under great mental strain and would naturally ascribe to the intruder the motive of rape."[7]

There was one remaining claim of error. Each of the other exceptions was predicated on the argument that John Winters' trial was unfair because of the evidence the court allowed the State to introduce. Exception 7 (that blood on the defendant's trousers had an innocent explanation) was the only instance in which defense lawyers argued that the trial was unfair because the court prohibited *the defense* from introducing evidence.

Attorney Bicknell devoted less than a page to the argument that Judge Thompson erred when he refused to allow the defense to show that blood on Winters' trousers could have come from his cut finger. He concluded with a sentence that was singularly unhelpful to the justices: "This principle is so elementary that it is difficult to cite precedent."[8]

Attorneys who appear before the Vermont Supreme Court often attach great weight to their oral arguments. But it is very rare for oral argument to alter an opinion formed by reading the briefs and trial record in advance of argument. When the author of a poorly written brief also argues the case, justices do not expect enlightenment.

Based on the briefing, the justices had no reason to believe that oral argument would alter opinions they had formed in reviewing the briefs and trial record. Whether the new lawyer for the defendant could enlighten the court remained to be seen. The supreme court docket entry for *State v. Winters* read "appearing for the defendant: Clarence Darrow (of Chicago, Ill.)."

⇒ 17 ⇐

Darrow Arrives

"WINTERS' CASE WAITS ARRIVAL OF DARROW," proclaimed the *Rutland Herald* on Monday, January 9, 1928. The Vermont Supreme Court's opening session for the New Year was to begin the next day. Argument in *State v. Winters* was set for Thursday. Lawyers, legislators, and reporters were already clamoring for courtroom seats.

The new supreme court building provided far more space than the previous cramped quarters in the State House, but court officers were planning to open the courtroom doors so the "large number of Montpelier citizens, including a generous proportion of women" could hear the famed attorney's voice.[1] Darrow's celebrity and impending appearance was a respite for weary Vermonters only two months removed from the devastating flood of November 1927.

The remaining supreme court terms of 1927 were canceled, although its building was not severely damaged. A few hundred yards away, the Washington County courthouse had more than thirteen feet of water in its vaults where court records were kept. Harrie Chase, the newest member of the court, was for a moment thought lost in the flood. His wife reported him missing, but he was aboard the *Ambassador*, a Central Vermont train stalled by floodwaters.[2]

The far greater consequence than the rumored loss of a supreme court justice was the very real wreckage the flood caused. If ever a state needed federal money to survive a natural disaster, it was when the flood of 1927 destroyed roads, bridges, and railroads—literally isolating rural Vermont. But President Coolidge was standing on principle.

Calvin Coolidge did not believe the federal government should help states recover from whatever havoc nature visited upon them. This policy was consistent with Coolidge's laissez-faire approach to governing. Unfortunately for Vermont, the president had just demonstrated his principle by refusing aid to southern states inundated by a record-breaking Mississippi flood.

When Vermont's governor, congressional delegation, and president of Vermont Marble Company made the difficult trip to Washington to plead for federal funds, Coolidge would not budge. At a press conference called in response to a growing demand for federal flood control appropriations, the president said it would not have done anything to alleviate the damage when "a quarter mile stretch of mountain slipped down into the road and cut off . . . the Union [part of the town of Plymouth] and where I live."[3]

Clarence Darrow, never a fan of Coolidge (he characterized him as "a small-sized New England politician" in private correspondence), prompted more amusement than resentment when he said publicly that "Calvin Coolidge is the greatest man ever to come out of Plymouth, Vermont."[4] It was a mark of Darrow's celebrity that when the "famous Chicago criminal lawyer" arrived in Montpelier, anything he did or said was news.

Vermonters knew that Darrow was here because he was fulfilling his son's promise to Winters' aunt Laura Cooley, but readers were eager to hear tidbits unrelated to the case. What did Clarence Darrow think of Vermont? ("He is an admirer of the beauty of the Green Mountains"). What about the crime wave in Chicago? ("No more pronounced than other large cities, though advertised more"). What did he have to say about his important cases? ("All cases are important").[5]

Newspaper editors prompted a debate about Darrow's motives as a criminal defense lawyer. The *Brattleboro Reformer* assailed him for "making a business of defending the country's most notorious criminals."[6] The St. Johnsbury *Caledonian Record* replied that if that was intended as a critique of Darrow's representation of John Winters, "it would be a shame . . . simply because of his fame as a criminal lawyer."[7] Clarence Darrow courted controversy. Americans were as familiar with his cases as they were with Lindbergh's flights or Chaplin's movies. When it was revealed that Darrow had received $65,000 for representing Loeb and Leopold, Darrow responded that he deserved $200,000.

Vermonters well knew Darrow's defense of evolution in the Scopes trial. "It's alright," wrote the *Middlebury Register*, "we're glad to have him with us, provided he doesn't start any monkey business."[8]

Darrow's arrival was tracked by reporters who asserted, accurately, that the celebrity had checked into the Pavilion Hotel, "with his wife" —an assumption. There was no doubt, however, that Darrow was preparing for the argument. He met with trial attorneys Herbert Tupper and Fred Bicknell, who had previously furnished Darrow with the trial transcript and their brief.

Clarence Darrow never underestimated the significance of trial publicity. Even before his arrival in Vermont, Darrow told reporters that there was not enough evidence to convict Winters "under ordinary circumstances." He contended that in the "hue and cry" that arose after the murder of Cecelia Gullivan, the State needed to "get somebody."[9] His statement fed the public's appetite for murder cases, but the Vermont Supreme Court would need to hear far better legal arguments if America's most famous defense attorney hoped to save the life of his client.

Chief Justice John Watson opened the January 1928 session of the supreme court in a courtroom "as fitting . . . as any supreme court room in this section of the country."[10] Vermonters were justly proud of the neoclassical style of a building free of "excess" and constructed less than a decade before of Barre granite that matched the adjacent State House. Excess was a word equally inappropriate to the justices of the court. Judicial robes were a relatively recent phenomenon, as were chairs that matched.[11]

But of greatest concern for lawyers arguing before the court was the chief justice's capacity to produce unanimous decisions. If ever there was disagreement among the justices about a decision's result or reasoning, Chief Justice Watson did not encourage dissenting (or even concurring) opinions.

That practice was particularly sobering to attorneys seeking reversals of criminal convictions. Clarence Darrow had little faith in the judicial process and even less in judges. His own experience had taught him that if judges were not corrupt or inept (or both), they almost always favored the prosecution. It was Darrow's extraordinary ability to sway juries that often balanced the uneven scale of justice.

Darrow was now within forty-eight hours of his appearance before a court without a jury. He was an attentive student as co-counsels Bicknell and Tupper briefed him on the composition of the five-member supreme court. The chief justice, who had served on the court since 1899, and three other justices were former prosecutors. Darrow did not have to be told that the court was likely to be more receptive to the argument of the attorney general of Vermont than the defense lawyer from Chicago.

But if Clarence Darrow needed any additional lesson about the challenge he confronted, it came on the opening day of the January term when the supreme court affirmed a murder conviction.[12] It was not the unanimity of *State v. Tubbs* that startled the lawyers for John Winters. It was that the opinion was written by Judge Frank Thompson, the trial judge in *State v. Winters*. Thompson had sat on the supreme court in the May 1927 term, substituting for a justice.

That the current members of the court thought highly enough of Thompson to assign him the opinion was not a good omen for Clarence Darrow. His appeal was premised on the argument that Judge Thompson committed errors in the trial so egregious that the supreme court should reverse a murder conviction in one of the most sensational cases in Vermont's history.

John Winters had either murdered Cecelia, or he had not. Unless the Vermont Supreme Court reversed his conviction, he would die in the electric chair. An innocent man could have no better lawyer than Clarence Darrow. And neither could a guilty one.

Reporters were almost as interested in the arrival of Winters as they were in Darrow's. The expectation was that Sheriff Fairbanks would transport the prisoner from Windsor State Prison early Thursday morning, the day of the appeal. The timing would again enable Wallis Fairbanks to portray himself as the sheriff who brought Winters to justice.

The sheriff, whose appeal of his own conviction was awaiting a decision of the supreme court, never missed an opportunity to link himself to *State v. Winters*. The previous July, Sheriff Fairbanks and State's Attorney Robert Twitchell—enforcing Prohibition when circumstances compelled them to—arrested James Romano. They had identified him as "the Italian fellow" who allegedly sold liquor to Winters on the evening before Cecelia Gullivan's murder.

Sheriff Fairbanks brought John Winters from state prison to the Woodstock courthouse to testify. The sheriff was mistaken if he believed his prisoner would assist the prosecution. Again before a Windsor County jury, the "clean-shaven, faultlessly dressed" Winters testified in a "cool, self-possessed manner as evident as it had been at the time of his trial."[13] Winters denied Romano was the man who sold him liquor. The defendant denied ever seeing Winters. Both were contradicted by other witnesses and the jury found Romano guilty.

It is likely that Winters' mother and aunt were present at that trial. It was a certainty that they would be at the supreme court. Maggie Winters and Laura Cooley came to Montpelier the day before the argument and were sharing a room at a boarding house. They had gotten word, perhaps from the prison warden, that John Winters would be arriving early as well.

An enterprising reporter, tipped that Winters might be transported the night before the argument, waited at Montpelier's railroad station. Shortly before midnight, he spotted Winters, whom he assumed would be shackled and in the custody of Sheriff Fairbanks. In fact, Winters was not manacled and was with state prison warden James McDermott. The reporter followed the warden and John Winters, "walking the streets without handcuffs [unrecognized] by persons on the streets."[14]

When John Winters reached the Montpelier jail, he saw his mother and aunt waiting for him. Mrs. Winters embraced "a son in trouble." When the reporter attempted to interview the defendant's mother, he was cut short by Mrs. Cooley, who was upset with newspaper accounts of the accident that killed her son. But each said they "had great confidence in the ability of Mr. Darrow."[15]

Confidence in Clarence Darrow was well-placed because they assumed, as did many others, that co-counsels Tupper and Bicknell would defer to America's greatest defense lawyer.

But if Herbert Tupper was willing to do so, apparently Fred Bicknell was not. Whatever the reason, the three-member defense team decided the appeal argument would be divided between Bicknell and Darrow.

There were some plausible explanations for the decision, each of which would have been advanced by Fred Bicknell. He could assert that he had carried a larger burden than Tupper at trial. He told Darrow that the Vermont Supreme Court expected attorneys before it to argue "the law not the facts." Bicknell was the primary author of the defense brief, and he suggested he was more prepared to argue Vermont law than his out-of-state co-counsel, irrespective of Mr. Darrow's eminence.

The supreme court ordinarily allowed each side one hour to argue. Splitting the time with Bicknell meant that Darrow would have only thirty minutes before the court. Herbert Tupper advised Bicknell to request the chief justice to extend the argument to two hours per side. Tupper tactfully suggested that Bicknell argue the first hour allotted to the defense. It was unnecessary to add that the last hour of argument to save the life of John Winters should be made by Clarence Darrow.

On Thursday morning, January 12, 1928, the robed justices filed to their seats behind the massive mahogany bench. Consistent with protocol, Chief Justice John Watson sat in the middle of the five-member court with the most junior justice, Harrie Chase, seated at the chief's far left. Watson had been on the supreme court for almost three decades, Chase for three months. When John Watson wrote his first supreme court opinion, Harrie Chase was ten years old.

They shared at least one common experience. Neither had ever seen so many persons in the courtroom of the Vermont Supreme Court. Nor had anyone else. "Never has such attention been attracted by a case before it," reported the *New York Times*. "Lawyers, state officials, and a large number of men and women crowded the room and stood in doorways."[16]

The defendant's mother and aunt were there but were not seated with him. John Winters sat to one side with Warden McDermott. "He is never shackled [and there is not] the slightest suggestion he is a prisoner. The chances are that eighty percent of those in court today were unable to identify him," said an observer.[17] Sheriff Wallis Fairbanks was there and made himself conspicuous by reminding reporters that he had been the one to arrest Winters.[18]

But all eyes were on one man. Spectators strained to get a glimpse of Clarence Darrow, who was seated with Tupper and Bicknell at counsel table. At precisely 10:00 a.m., the case was called by the court clerk. Fred Bicknell stood and asked Chief Justice Watson permission to allow Darrow, who was not admitted to practice in Vermont, to appear before the court.

There was no question that permission would be granted but when the chief justice did so, Darrow arose and bowed to the court. It was an unexpected gesture and enabled those in the courtroom to more fully view the famous lawyer before he resumed his seat. "A big, broad-shouldered man, slightly stooped, whose rugged face is heavily lined," wrote an observer.[19]

The next good look at Darrow would not come until late afternoon. As planned, Fred Bicknell requested the court to allow each side two hours of argument. Hearing no objection from the State, the chief justice granted the request. Bicknell opened for the defense.

As was often the case with Fred Bicknell, the logic of his approach was obscure. Even Sheriff Fairbanks, not noted for his attention to nuance, had commented how unusual it was to be asked to bring trial court exhibits to Montpelier.[20] The use of trial exhibits in supreme court argument is rarely permitted. It was not clear to the sheriff why Bicknell had made the request, and it became even less obvious to the justices during Bicknell's presentation.

Whatever the shortcomings of Fred Bicknell as a lawyer, he was a consummate professional when contrasted with Windsor County State's Attorney Robert Twitchell, who made the State's opening argument. Also at the State's counsel table was Special Prosecutor Raymond Trainor. But the second hour of the State's argument to uphold the murder conviction would be made by Attorney General J. Ward Carver. Trainor was a better lawyer than Carver, but the attorney general was running for reelection in November.

Attorney General Carver opened the afternoon session of argument. He concluded his allotted hour at 3:00 p.m. The climactic moment of the "profound sensation created last June when Clarence Darrow brought fresh hope to the friends and relatives of John Winters" had arrived.[21] "You have one hour and nineteen minutes for your argument, Mr. Darrow," intoned Chief Justice Watson.[22] Bicknell had not used his full hour, but Watson was making it clear to America's most famous lawyer that it was the chief justice's courtroom.

Clarence Darrow began his argument to the Vermont Supreme Court "with a voice so perfectly pitched that it easily carried" to the crowded hallway outside the courtroom.[23] Darrow noted his unfamiliarity with Vermont legal practice: "I endeavored to study the record, only to be informed that in this hearing it was a matter of law applying to exceptions taken at the trial."[24] It was, of course, Fred Bicknell who advised Darrow that he had to argue "law not facts."

It was obviously poor advice. "I make this statement now because counsel have spent most of their time arguing facts," said an irritated Darrow. He provided a salient example of a "fact argument" he would make had he been informed he could do so: "Why did Mrs. Pandjiris not identify Winters until two days after the attack?"[25]

Constrained by the advice of his co-counsel, Darrow's "dignified and scholarly argument held to the line of legal argument rather than recital of fact."[26] But that did not foreclose Clarence Darrow from making an argument that raised a question he sensed might be shared by some justices: did John Winters receive a fair trial?

There were two primary issues in Darrow's legal argument: Judge Thompson committed reversible error in allowing the prosecution to present evidence of the assault at the Evarts house, and in denying the defense the opportunity to submit evidence that blood on the defendant's trousers could have come from a cut finger. But before he reached those issues, Clarence Darrow wanted the justices to know how outrageous he thought the conduct of the trial had been.

Darrow claimed he had never heard of a trial court allowing a jury to see as an exhibit a recreation of the victim's bloody bed, calling it "a theatrical gimmick that has no place in a court of justice."[27] Darrow was not above making statements for purely dramatic effect. But when he said the exhibit was made to "madden and craze the jury," his aim was to remind the justices what they surely knew.[28] Special Prosecutor Trainor had used Cecelia Gullivan's severed head for exactly that purpose.

"Law is not a system of tricks," asserted Darrow.[29] Yet there must have been a part of him that admired the trial "tricks" of Raymond Trainor (Darrow would have said "strategies" if he had devised them). By shaping the evidence to suggest that Gullivan's murderer was intent on rape, the special prosecutor was then able to persuade the trial court judge that evidence of the assault on Mrs. Pandjiris was admissible to show Winters' motive and identity.

Darrow argued strenuously that there was no evidence of rape. "Any one of the twelve blows to her head could have killed her. The intruder was there to murder not rape."[30] But Darrow's courtroom experience and instinct for knowing when he was persuasive must have told him that it was time to move his other primary claim of legal error—the blood-on-the-trousers evidence.

At trial, defense counsel Bicknell was asked by Judge Thompson if he could show that the blood came from the defendant's finger. Bicknell had responded, "No, but we can show there was an opportunity." When Darrow began to argue this issue, he started with a statement that must have made his co-counsel feel somewhat better: "Mr. Bicknell said what any honest lawyer would say." Unsaid, was what Darrow was surely thinking—a better answer would have been "Yes, we can show it."

But now, Darrow exhibited the skill that made him an extraordinary lawyer. The prosecution had argued that Winters never noticed blood on his trousers the night before the murder. Nor did the defendant ever claim that he might have gotten blood on his trousers when he severed his finger. In fact, Winters' answer to the last question of Special Prosecutor Trainor's withering cross-examination, "You don't know where you got that blood on your trousers, do you John?" was "No."

"I don't care what Winters said to the prosecutor. I don't care if Winters did not notice blood on his trousers," exclaimed Darrow. "The State brings in trousers to have the jury infer it is the blood of the dead girl. Prove it? No! No one could prove it was her blood."[31] The prosecution and Darrow's co-counsel were seeing a glimpse of what made Darrow a great trial lawyer. The entire courtroom could see the difference Darrow might have made if he had represented Winters at trial.

Darrow did not maintain, as less gifted attorneys would have, that *the defendant* had a right to introduce evidence of an alternative explanation for the source of the blood on his trousers. Darrow made a more subtle argument. He argued *the jury* had a right to it: "Blood is important in a murder case. I don't know what the jury would have done with it, but the jury had a right to it."[32]

"There was not a sound in the courtroom" as Clarence Darrow closed his argument. "I am convinced that no defendant could have had a fair trial under these frightful circumstances. I submit that for the abundant error in the record this conviction should be reversed."[33] With that, the famed attorney picked up his papers and made his way from the courtroom to the adjacent Pavilion Hotel. At the entrance stood Mrs. Margaret Winters and Mrs. Laura Cooley to thank him.

They may have asked Darrow when to expect a decision, but the Vermont lawyers had a much better idea of how long it would take for the Vermont Supreme Court to issue an opinion in a first-degree murder case. Tupper and Bicknell would have told the women and John Winters that the court could issue an opinion within thirty days and would in no event take longer than six months.

They were wrong.

⇒ 18 ⇐

Deadlock

W HEN LAWYERS Herbert Tupper and Fred Bicknell advised Clarence Darrow to expect a decision of the Vermont Supreme Court in *State v Winters* within one to six months, they were sharing the conventional wisdom of past practice. But by 1928, a Vermonter had already made "conventional wisdom" suspect. In August 1927, Calvin Coolidge handed slips of paper to reporters gathered at the dedication of Mount Rushmore that read, "I do not choose to run for President in nineteen twenty-eight."[1]

In the year that followed Coolidge's stunning declaration, the phrase "do not choose" was parsed by many who believed the president's single sentence deviously kept open a "draft Coolidge" window.[2] Coolidge *did* choose. His presidency would end in March 1929. Long enough—though none then knew it—for Calvin Coolidge to make a decision that would alter the fate of John Winters.

The Vermont Supreme Court's January 1928 term was noteworthy for more than just Clarence Darrow's appearance. As the first postflood term, it was a busy docket. Appeals were heard in sixteen cases in addition to the daylong argument in *Winters*. It was the first full term for the Vermont Bar's wunderkind, Harrie Chase, who had climbed to the top of the state's judicial ladder with unprecedented speed.

Only thirty-eight when appointed to the court by Governor John Weeks in September 1927 (the second youngest justice in the court's history), Harrie Chase was a trial judge at twenty-nine and chief trial judge at thirty-five. Chase was joining a court where the youngest justice was over fifty, two were in their sixties, and the chief justice was exactly twice as old as the new justice. Chief Justice John Watson's duty was to ensure members kept up with the caseload, so he welcomed the addition of youthful energy to the court.

The focus of lawyers Tupper and Bicknell on the January term was not limited to their appearance on behalf of John Winters nor the debut of Justice Chase. Another opinion handed down by the court in January was of special interest given the challenge they and Darrow faced in persuading a majority of the court that Winters should be granted a new trial.

Although *State v. Fairbanks* had no bearing on the legal issues in the Winters appeal, it contained clues—pointing in different directions—for those speculating about the outcome of the Winters case. Sheriff Wallis Fairbanks' appeal had been heard by the full court, including Justice Chase, in the truncated November 1927 term.

The opinion reversing the sheriff's conviction for adultery lacked competent legal analysis. The jury had found credible the testimony of the two state wards who testified to having sexual relations with the sheriff. But Justice Sherman R. Moulton writing for the court said greater cross-examination should have been allowed when the principal witnesses were "young women of almost equal depravity."[3]

Clarence Darrow, in oral argument, identified sworn testimony of Fairbanks (that smudges on Gullivan's sleeping porch wall were footprints) as particularly problematic. The court's reversal of the sheriff's conviction suggested that justices had a more benign view of his veracity. But not all justices. The opinion contained a line rarely seen during Chief Justice Watson's tenure: "A *majority* of this Court holds . . . a reversal is required"[4] (emphasis added).

Conventional wisdom held that the opinions of the Vermont Supreme Court were always unanimous. But Calvin Coolidge had already guaranteed that 1928 would be unconventional.

It is unlikely that Clarence Darrow gave any thought to how long it might take the Vermont Supreme Court to reach a decision in *State v. Winters*. His January 1928 appearance certainly fulfilled Paul's pledge to Laura Cooley. Darrow embarked on a speaking tour in the New Year, debating proponents of capital punishment and raising money for the National Association for the Advancement of Colored People. He saw no reason to alter his initial appraisal of the Winters case to Paul: "It is doubtful if anything can be done."[5]

Darrow's defense of John Winters before the Vermont Supreme Court was a speck in the famed lawyer's legal career, but his appearance transformed an already sensational murder case into the most publicized criminal case appeal in the court's history. Chief Justice John Watson's thirty years on the court left little doubt among Vermont lawyers about which justice would write the opinion in *State v. Winters*. It would be the chief.

John Watson was born in 1851, making him too young to serve in the Civil War. But in 1883, Watson, serving as an officer in the Vermont National Guard, led the Bradford militia on an overnight march to Fairlee, recapturing a powder house held by striking copper miners at Ely.[6] His reputation for leadership was matched by his reputation for studiousness. Though Watson had no formal education beyond common school and the academy (he "read" for the law), his exposition on the Vermont Constitution and slavery before the Vermont Bar Association in 1921 is a significant essay more than a century after he wrote it.[7]

Lawyers Tupper and Bicknell had already assumed the chief justice would author the opinion in *State v. Winters*—an instance of conventional wisdom being correct. They were more interested in calculating how rapidly the court would decide cases heard in January. It was the court's practice to issue opinions at the start of a term. The next term was in February. The defense attorneys knew that if the court decided quickly in *State v. Winters* it would almost certainly be a unanimous opinion affirming the conviction.

In February, the court did decide a January appeal involving John Winters. It upheld the conviction of James Romano for unauthorized sale of intoxicating liquor to Winters on the evening before Cecelia Gullivan's murder.[8] It did not escape the court's notice that a Windsor County jury had again disbelieved the sworn testimony of Winters. It was a unanimous opinion, as were two other January cases—a dispute over a real estate agent's commission and a claim of damages for a railroad's delay in delivering bananas.[9]

The next scheduled supreme court term of 1928 was set for May. Fourteen cases from January remained undecided including the Winters appeal and another case of "a most vicious and inhuman killing."[10] Conventional wisdom anticipated the May term would bring decisions in both murder cases. Indeed, the addition of the youthful Justice Chase to Chief Justice Watson's reputation for efficiency suggested that the court might hand down opinions disposing of all January appeals.

The first week of May 1928 brought a glimpse of spring to Vermonters who had endured a bitter postflood winter. The supreme court opened its term on May 2. Defense attorneys Tupper and Bicknell advised John Winters to expect a decision any day of the week. The lawyers had good news—for another client—on day one.

Justice Harrie Chase's first written opinion reversed the illegal sale of intoxicating liquor conviction of a defendant whose appeal had been argued by Tupper and Bicknell in the January term. The case was prosecuted by Windsor County State's Attorney Robert Twitchell with Judge Frank Thompson presiding. Writing for a unanimous court, Justice Chase chided the prosecutor for "so lacking in [his] failure to bring us a record of what [he] said we cannot perceive . . . [his] claim."[11] Whatever delight Tupper and Bicknell had in learning that Justice Chase shared their view of State's Attorney Twitchell's incompetence was small comfort to John Winters. He awaited notice of a decision that could mean his next journey would be from his death cell to the chair in the adjacent chamber. Two days later, his lawyers did have news for him.

On May 4, the supreme court handed down its opinion in *State v. Lapan*, the other murder case argued in January. The decision, written by Justice George Powers, second in seniority to the chief justice, affirmed the defendant's conviction for second-degree murder. The court's opinion included a legal analysis disconcerting to Winters' lawyers.

In *Lapan*, the trial court admitted the State's evidence of an exhibit with blood on it. As in *Winters*, the State's expert could not identify the victim as the source of the blood nor even that it was human blood. The defendant's lawyer sought to show that the blood on the State's exhibit (a floorboard taken from defendant's car) may have come from a cut on the defendant's dog. The trial judge refused to admit the defendant's evidence. A unanimous supreme court upheld the trial judge's ruling.

Justice Powers described the facts of the murder as "brutal and distressing."[12] It was difficult to envision how the justices could view the horrific details of Cecelia Gullivan's murder as anything less. It was now a near certainty that Chief Justice Watson would write the opinion deciding the most significant capital case in the court's history. Many lawyers, including Tupper and Kendall, believed the chief had already written it.

Yet to their collective disbelief, Winters' lawyers watched the weeks of the May term pass without a decision in *State v. Winters*. The supreme court handed down opinions in eight appeals that had been argued in the January 1928 term and nine more that were heard in February. Among those opinions were four reversals written by Justice Harrie Chase.

Attorney General J. Ward Carver's biennial report for the two years ending June 30, 1928, noted, "All of the homicide cases tried by jury have been disposed of in the higher court without reversal except one which was argued in the January term of the Supreme Court and is still pending."[13]

As spring stretched into summer without a decision, there was increasing conjecture that Chief Justice Watson was confronted with a court where he could not ensure unanimity. Whether this meant the chief was dealing with a single justice or a more divided court could only be guessed. But the most recent change in the supreme court's composition was the addition of Justice Harrie Chase.

In July 1928, the supreme court issued a decision diminishing speculation that the chief justice was dealing with a divided court. In *Leonard v. Willcox, et al.*, justices faced the "delicate matter [of determining] whether a judge is so biased or prejudiced that he cannot administer impartial justice."[14] "Delicate matter" put it politely. Chief Trial Judge Julius Willcox was next in line to be a supreme court justice if a vacancy on the court arose.

Judge Willcox was accused of bias in a child custody case where his prejudice against the mother prompted him to grant an abusive father visitation rights even when the court no longer had jurisdiction. The supreme court noted the mother's claim of "indecent conduct by her former husband (the prurient details of which we omit)."[15]

"This is a matter which does not alone concern the parties . . . The courts, in the eyes of the public, should be . . . free . . . from even the suspicion of partiality," declared a unanimous supreme court.[16] The decision prohibited Chief Trial Judge Willcox from further participation in the child custody case. If ever there was a decision justices wished to avoid, it was one that labeled a potential supreme court colleague as biased.

The unanimity of the justices appeared to indicate that Chief Justice Watson could count on colleagues to follow his lead. Attorneys Tupper and Bicknell reverted to conventional wisdom. *State v. Winters* and the four other undecided cases from the January term would likely be unanimous and would certainly be issued at the start of the October 1928 term.

On October 3, 1928, the Vermont Supreme Court handed down four opinions: a contract case; a claim for unlawful cutting of trees; an insurance case; and a claim for damages arising from an automobile accident. Each decision was unanimous. The decisions disposed of every appeal argued in the January 1928 term—except one.

No decision in *State v Winters*. There was now no need for conjecture or conventional wisdom. Anyone could do the math. On the question of whether the conviction of John Winters for the murder of Cecelia Gullivan should be upheld, four justices were deadlocked: two would affirm and two would reverse.

Why hadn't the fifth justice—whoever it might be—reached a decision? It was unprecedented. Chief Justice Watson could not—and would not—allow a justice to escape the responsibility of deciding the most significant criminal appeal in his three decades on the Vermont Supreme Court.

But the chief had never been on the court with someone half his age.

⇒ 19 ⇐

Wunderkind

THE VERMONT AUTUMN of 1928 may have brought disquieting news of a stymied supreme court, but it also prompted the return of its most famous son. In September, President Calvin Coolidge left Washington aboard the Presidential Special to tour his native state. It was his chance to make amends for his "benign neglect" of the consequences of Vermont's devastating flood of 1927.[1]

The president's train made twelve stops as it crisscrossed the state on reconstructed tracks and bridges. Vermonters were universally welcoming, and it may have been the warmth of his reception that prompted Coolidge to use his last stop in Bennington to make remarks from the rear of the train. His tribute to "the brave little state of Vermont" would be remembered long after his natural disaster policy was forgotten.

When Coolidge said "Vermont is a state I love," it reflected his faith in the Vermonters on whom he relied in his presidency. Traveling with the president on the "Special" was John Garibaldi Sargent ("Gary" to the president). In March 1925, Sargent, who had served as Vermont's attorney general, received a cryptic message from the Coolidge White House: come immediately to Washington without telling anyone.[2]

Coolidge had just been inaugurated on March 4 after his overwhelming electoral victory of November 1924. One week into his "own" presidency he faced a political crisis when the United States Senate rejected his nominee for attorney general. It was the first time the Senate had failed to confirm a president's attorney general nominee since Andrew Johnson's candidate was voted down in the bitter aftermath of the president's impeachment.

For Coolidge, it was a quick lesson in the vagaries of presidential power—and in the untrustworthiness of his vice president, who would have been the tie-breaking vote for confirmation but claimed to have "overslept." President Coolidge did not intend it to happen again. "I am going to nominate you to be attorney general of the United States," he told a startled John Sargent, who had arrived in Washington without appropriate clothes.[3]

Attorney General Sargent was a steady presence for Coolidge, who took comfort from a Vermonter sitting next to him in cabinet meetings. It was not the first time he relied on "Gary." When young Calvin Coolidge arrived at Ludlow's Black River Academy, another Plymouth farm boy was there. Twelve years older, the 6'3" 250-pound John Sargent guaranteed that slender Calvin would not be hazed.[4]

The Presidential Special made a stop at Ludlow, where the two alums paid a visit to the academy. Though Coolidge and Sargent would remain in office until March 1929, their trip to Vermont was a recognition of the Coolidge presidency ending. Herbert Hoover was the Republican nominee for president and there was little doubt that he would ride the wave of "Coolidge prosperity" to victory in November 1928.

Sargent had made perfunctory appearances on behalf of Hoover. Coolidge was even less enthusiastic. The attorney general saw the difference between the two men when he and Secretary of Commerce Hoover were sent by Coolidge to Vermont in November 1927 to survey flood damage. When Hoover's car became mired in mud, others got out to push. The secretary of commerce remained in the car. Vermonters knew their president would have pushed.[5]

Herbert Hoover easily defeated the Democrat's nominee, New York Governor Al Smith. Clarence Darrow spent much of the fall campaigning for Smith who, as the first Catholic presidential candidate and a "wet" on prohibition, stood almost no chance of election. Darrow gave little thought to the Winters appeal.

Chief Justice John Watson (and John Winters) could think of little else. It was likely that Watson had written and circulated a draft opinion in *State v. Winters* to his colleagues before the May 1928 term. It was equally probable that the chief's draft affirmed the conviction of John Winters for the murder of Cecelia Gullivan. By its October term, the court had issued decisions disposing of every appeal argued in January 1928 except *State v. Winters*.

Herbert Tupper and Fred Bicknell kept Winters, his mother, and his aunt apprised of the status of the case. But the attorneys had no better idea than the defendant of when a decision might come or why it was delayed. Chief Justice Watson could not answer the first question, but he knew the answer to the second.

Justice Harrie Chase would not decide. The chief justice had been looking for a majority to affirm the conviction of John Winters. That was now secondary to persuading the newest and youngest justice on the Vermont Supreme Court to decide one way or another and break the deadlock of a divided court. The Vermont Supreme Court handed down seven opinions in its November term. *State v. Winters* was not among them.

In November 1928, Vermonters reelected Attorney General J. Ward Carver. Windsor County voters replaced State's Attorney Robert Twitchell with Lawrence Edgerton. Sheriff Wallis Fairbank did not seek reelection. Despite extensive cross-examination on retrial of the "depraved" young women Fairbanks claimed were lying when they testified he had sex with them, the sheriff was again convicted of adultery. The jury returned a guilty verdict in twelve minutes.[6]

The court opened 1929 by handing down eleven unanimous decisions, each disposing of appeals that had been argued in the last ninety days. One opinion again upheld an award of damages for delay in delivering bananas. "This case has been here once before," noted the court.[7] But there was nothing said about the case Clarence Darrow argued in January 1928.

By 1929, President Calvin Coolidge was the lamest of ducks. "There is another atmosphere different from the Coolidge atmosphere," said an observer who claimed vigorous President-elect Hoover would get more done than Theodore Roosevelt.[8] Senators and business leaders who lobbied Coolidge over each of the scores of federal judges he had appointed turned their attention to the new administration.

Calvin Coolidge's policy of leaving states on their own to respond to natural disasters was detrimental to Vermont, but he "demonstrated his genuine interest in Vermont by designating Vermonters for places of responsibility."[9] In January, the departing president was preparing to reward his native state with "one last generous act."[10] Coolidge intended to nominate a Vermonter to a court that—excepting the United States Supreme Court—was the most important tribunal in the nation.

The United States Court of Appeals for the Second Circuit is responsible for appeals made from the federal trial courts within its "circuit"— the states of New York, Connecticut, and Vermont. Although it was then one of nine circuit courts in the United States, its significance far exceeded other courts of appeals because cases dealing with the most powerful business interests in America, including Wall Street, were decided by judges of the Second Circuit.[11]

In the history of the Second Circuit there had never been a Vermonter on the court. It was not for lack of trying. In 1923, John Sargent, representing the Vermont Bar, met with President Warren Harding's attorney general, Harry Daugherty, to urge the appointment of a Vermonter to a vacancy on the court. The meeting was arranged by Earle Kinsley, an active member of the Vermont Republican Party.

Kinsley introduced Sargent to the corrupt Daugherty with the remark that "Vermont has never been represented on the court of appeals." The attorney general replied, "What did the Vermont delegation do for us [at the 1920 Republican convention] in Chicago?"[12] Vermont had cast its vote for another candidate even after Warren Harding secured the nomination. It was a quick lesson in politics for John Sargent.

By 1929, Attorney General Sargent did not need lessons. At his urging, Congress enacted legislation adding a fifth judge to the Second Circuit. President Coolidge signed the new law in January. In Earle Kinsley's recounting, the judicial vacancy came to Sargent's attention only when his special assistant said, "Wouldn't this be a good time to appoint a man from Vermont, General?"[13]

Kinsley's account would ring true only to those who had recently fallen off a hay wagon. The attorney general's special assistant was Paul Chase, Harrie's younger brother. When Sargent left Vermont to take charge of the Department of Justice in 1925, he offered the position to Paul. Four years later, Attorney General Sargent was making plans that delighted their father and his great friend, Brattleboro lawyer Charles Chase.

Sargent was returning to a private practice that promised to be lucrative because of his four years as the nation's attorney general. Paul Chase, who had served four years as his special assistant, would be a partner in the new firm. The attorney general had an even better plan for Paul's brother.

John Sargent almost certainly spoke with Harrie Chase about the newly created vacancy on the Second Circuit before the Vermont Supreme Court began its January term. It was essential for Sargent to receive assurance from Chase in advance of the attorney general's meeting with President Coolidge that Chase would leave the Vermont Supreme Court if nominated and confirmed to the federal bench.

Even for a lame duck president there was pressure to nominate a candidate favored by New York interests to the prestigious Second Circuit. A delegation of prominent New York lawyers bearing a petition signed by former Chief Justice Charles Evans Hughes with the name of their preferred choice scheduled a meeting with President Coolidge. They were a day late.[14]

Judge Chase was candid in later years about the reason Coolidge nominated him: the attorney general was a friend of the family.[15] The friend and the family knew that if confirmed by the US Senate, Justice Chase would be leaving the Vermont Supreme Court.

They knew more than Chief Justice Watson. Harrie Chase sat on the court as it began its January 1929 term. As with each of the justices, the chief assigned him the responsibility for writing the court's opinion in designated cases.[16] Watson pressed Justice Chase to make a decision in *State v. Winters*. Harrie Chase would never have to decide.

The Associated Press broke the story: "Harrie B. Chase of Vermont Supreme Court Nominated for U.S. Circuit Judge."[17] The chief justice was not the only one surprised. A joint session of the Vermont Legislature was about to convene to "retain" five supreme court justices. The pro forma vote was to confirm the court's current members: Chief Justice Watson, Justices George Powers, Sherman R. Moulton, Leighton P. Slack, and Harrie Chase.

But President Coolidge's nomination of Chase to the US Court of Appeals had yet to be confirmed by the US Senate. The dilemma was well put by the *Burlington Free Press*: "Unless this [immediately] takes place, the Vermont Legislature will be forced to defer the election of the justices a few days (for which there is no precedent) or run the risk of leaving Justice Chase jobless should his federal appointment fail of confirmation in the Senate."[18]

Harrie Chase was undoubtedly urged to resign immediately. Despite assurance from Vermont Senator Porter Dale that he would be easily confirmed, Justice Chase refused entreaties to surrender his seat on the Vermont Supreme Court in advance of Senate confirmation.[19]

On the last day of January 1929, the Senate approved President Coolidge's nomination of the first Vermonter to serve on the US Court of Appeals for the Second Circuit.

The confirmation ended Chase's sixteen months on the Vermont Supreme Court. Not yet forty, he would be one of the youngest court of appeals judges in the nation's history. Judge Chase, said an observer, "stands a good chance of taking the last remaining step [to] the Supreme Court of the land."[20]

"A great victory for Vermont," proclaimed Senator Dale. Justice Chase "has had a splendid record on the Vermont bench. He is still young," said Vermont Congressman Elbert Brigham.[21] His last sentence was true.

Wunderkind had ascended. *State v. Winters* remained undecided.

⇒ 20 ⇐

"The Peculiar Circumstances"

JUSTICE HARRIE CHASE submitted his formal letter of resignation to Governor John Weeks on February 2, 1929. A joint session of the Vermont Legislature was scheduled to elect a justice to fill the Chase vacancy. In conformance with the rigid seniority system, the next vacancy on the Vermont Supreme Court was to be filled by the most senior trial judge: Chief Trial Judge Julius Willcox.

The near-sacred principle of seniority was embedded in the selection of supreme court justices. Judges were elected by the legislature and ascended in lockstep up the judicial ladder from most junior trial judge to chief trial judge to—if the fates were favorable—the Vermont Supreme Court.[1] The rapid rise of Harrie Chase owed as much to fate as talent.

Eight months earlier, the justices of the supreme court had disqualified Judge Willcox from a child custody case because of his bias. Whether it was for that reason or others, now "a substantial movement was underway to elect Judge Thompson."[2] Frank Thompson was second in seniority to Julius Willcox.

When support for Thompson appeared to be growing, "there was considerable speculation as to Judge Thompson's attitude. No one professed to really know whether he instigated the movement on his behalf or tacitly agreed to the unusual procedure or opposed it altogether."[3] Julius Willcox would have made it his business to know.

If Frank Thompson opposed the effort "altogether," he took his time in telling Willcox. Those who backed Thompson could not overcome the legislature's custom of filling a supreme court vacancy with the most senior trial judge, and "supporters of Judge Willcox severely ruptured the plan."[4] On February 7, 1929, legislators approved Willcox's move up the judicial ladder.

Justice Willcox made a statement to the press: "Although my position comes as a routine replacement to fill a vacancy, I am deeply grateful to my friends and others for their support."[5] "Routine" was not a word that described the vacancy, the replacement, nor the first murder case the new justice would hear.

Chief Justice John Watson had ordered reargument in *State v. Winters*. It would be up to Justice Julius Willcox to decide if the Vermont Supreme Court should reverse the conviction of John Winters for the murder of Ceclia Gullivan because of an error made by Judge Frank Thompson.

The court's order directed lawyers for the defendant and the State to confine their arguments to a single claim of error ("Exception 7"): whether Judge Thompson erred in refusing to allow the defendant's attorney to introduce evidence that the blood on Winters' trousers could have come from his finger cut. The clerk's notice to the parties set the argument for March 7.

Defense attorney Herbert Tupper conveyed the news to the two people with the most at stake: John Winters and Clarence Darrow. It was a "good news/bad news" message, though it was only Winters who needed an explanation. The good news was obvious—the Supreme Court was divided on an issue that could result in his conviction being reversed. The bad news for Winters was that the court had already decided without the need for a fifth justice that the other six claims of error were insufficient reason to reverse his conviction for murder.

The most significant question for Winters (and for Tupper) was whether Clarence Darrow would make another appearance in *State v. Winters*. Even Laura Cooley conceded that Darrow's first argument before the Vermont Supreme Court fulfilled the promise Paul Darrow had made to her after little Harry's death. Yet as Darrow was to remark when asked about his commitment, "Once I get into a case I never quit as long as my health is good enough to keep going."[6]

Unspoken was Clarence Darrow's "insane desire" to preserve the life of a defendant who faced capital punishment. Supreme court clerk Joseph Frantini received a written request from Darrow. Would the court be willing to reschedule *State v. Winters* for March 8 instead of March 7 so he could take part in the reargument? The justices met in conference to consider the request.

"Court Changes Day to Suit Darrow," proclaimed the *Brattleboro Reformer*. One can only guess whether Chief Justice Watson embraced the idea. But he could not take issue with the *Reformer*'s explanation of the reason for Darrow's request: "It was argued once with Mr. Darrow present but . . . Harrie Chase . . . left the case in such a position that a reargument was necessary."[7]

When the Vermont Supreme Court met Friday, March 8, 1929, to hear reargument in *State v. Winters* much had changed in the fourteen months since the first argument and much had not. The court had a new justice, and the country had a new president. (Herbert Hoover was inaugurated on March 4.) Fred Bicknell, former co-counsel for Winters, had just been elected to the trial judge vacancy that occurred when Julius Willcox moved up the judicial ladder.

John Winters was again in the courtroom, transported from the Windsor State Prison death cell where he had been confined since November 1926. His mother and aunt attended the hearing, squeezed into a gallery "overflowing with spectators . . . with long lines of people standing in the corridors of the building."[8] Clarence Darrow was still a celebrity.

Two lawyers who had argued portions of the first appeal in January 1928 (Fred Bicknell for Winters and Windsor County State's Attorney Robert Twitchell for the State) were no longer participants. Chief Justice Watson limited oral argument to an hour per side. Freed of Bicknell's participation, Herbert Tupper and Darrow easily divided their allotted hour. Tupper would open with fifteen minutes of argument, reserving forty-five minutes for Darrow, who would close the argument after Attorney General J. Ward Carver made the State's presentation.

Tupper provided Darrow with as much insight as he could into Julius Willcox. He had often appeared before trial Judge Willcox and Tupper would have told Darrow about the attempt of Judge Frank Thompson's supporters to block the new justice's path to the supreme court.

Darrow admired Herbert Tupper and may have found his perspective useful, but nothing could supplant the foundation of every Clarence Darrow appeal to judge, justice, or jury: his instinct for what troubled his listeners. His sense that some justices were concerned about the fairness of the defendant's trial prompted his focus on the blood evidence in his first appearance before the court. ("Blood is important in a murder case. I don't know what the jury would have done with it, but they had a right to it.")[9]

A deadlocked Vermont Supreme Court's order to the parties to reargue only "Exception 7" was testament to Darrow's unerring insight. Attorney General Carver read from the trial transcript, reiterating the State's contention that Judge Thompson's refusal to admit the blood evidence was proper. The attorney general's argument was deemed "effective" by observers, but that was not the argument those in the court, outside the court, and on the court were awaiting.[10]

"Eager to catch every word," spectators strained to hear "Clarence Darrow of Chicago" as he rose again to plead the case of a defendant sentenced to death.[11] "His voice tinged with a soft drawl, his clothes slightly disheveled and old fashioned," he looked "very much like a country lawyer."[12] Darrow knew he was arguing to a single justice.

In "an eloquent appeal for a new trial for John Winters," Darrow again argued that it was prejudicial error for the trial court to deny the jury the opportunity to hear that the blood on Winters' trousers could have an explanation consistent with the presumption of innocence.[13]

He emphasized what might trouble a new justice who, for a variety of reasons, could have doubts about Judge Thompson. "This conviction," asserted the nation's greatest defense lawyer, "was based on circumstantial evidence without a single trace of fact."[14]

With the close of arguments, Chief Justice Watson stood and, consistent with protocol, led the justices in single file to the court's adjacent conference room. The justices took their places around the conference table. Each justice—the new justice most of all—knew why they were there. The chief justice wanted the Vermont Supreme Court to decide *State v. Winters*.

Watson would have provided Justice Willcox with the chief's draft opinion affirming the conviction, likely written by May 1928, four months after Darrow's first appearance. The other justices had already agreed with Watson that none of the first six exceptions were errors that compelled reversal. Exception 7 remained undecided. Chief Justice Watson asked the new justice the question he repeatedly asked Justice Harrie Chase: Have you decided?

Justice Willcox said he had.

Clarence Darrow was leaving the courtroom when a reporter caught up with him and learned that "the world-famous criminal lawyer was on his way to Montreal en route to his home in Chicago."[15] Darrow was traveling on the *Ambassador*, Central Vermont Railway's express. It was the same train on which Justice Harrie Chase was located after being reported missing in the 1927 flood.

"What do you think of Vermont?" asked the reporter. It was a question to a celebrity, not an attorney. "Vermont," Mr. Darrow declared "is a glorious state . . . Your hills with their mantle of snow are a sight that I will long recall with pleasure."[16] Clarence Darrow was not planning on coming back.

He may not even have reached Chicago when the *New York Times* reported he would have reason to return. "Darrow Keeps Pledge by Saving Man's Life," proclaimed the *Times*, seventy-two hours after his argument. "He has snatched from the shadow of the electric chair John Winters . . . By a vote of 3-2, the Vermont Supreme Court granted a new trial to Winters."[17]

The *Rutland Herald* asserted: "Julius Willcox, baby member of the Supreme Court, is being credited with casting the deciding vote in the Winters case . . . [on] the point of the bloodstains on which Clarence Darrow made his strong argument . . . his decision was made pretty quick."[18]

So "quick" that the court majority (Willcox joined Justices Powers and Moulton) did not issue a written opinion with their decision. The extraordinary departure from the supreme court's procedure could only have come at the chief justice's direction. Watson had waited long enough for a decision. He was not going to wait for the majority to write an opinion.

Ten days after announcing the decision, the court filed its lengthy opinion in *State v. Winters*. It was not written by the majority. It was written by Chief Justice Watson. "The writer of this opinion, and Mr. Justice Slack think that the seventh exception . . . [must] be resolved against the [defendant]. The majority of the Court, however, thinks otherwise."[19]

The chief justice asserted, in unusually critical language, that reversal of the conviction of John Winters for the murder of Cecelia Gullivan could only be reached by "disregarding . . . rules . . . and making presumptions . . . against the trial court for which there is no warrant in the rules of law or practice."[20]

The three justices in the majority were sensitive to the chief justice's criticism that they had disregarded precedent and practice in deciding that Winters' attorney had made a proper offer of the defendant's blood evidence. "The majority does not in any way recede from former holdings regarding the sufficiency of offers of evidence but simply says [no further offer was required] *in the peculiar circumstances of this case*"[21] (emphasis added).

The case of *State v. Winters* could be described in many ways, including "peculiar."

Almost any word would fit—except "closed."

⇒ 21 ⇐

Winters' Time

THE VERMONT SUPREME COURT'S OPINION in *State v. Winters* was released on March 22, 1929. There was little interest in learning how the court reached the result. Reporters, lawyers, and John Winters had only one question about the case: Would Clarence Darrow represent the defendant in the retrial for the murder of Cecelia Gullivan?

The answer was not long in coming. Clarence Darrow spent his seventy-second birthday, April 18, in Windsor State Prison. Darrow and Herbert Tupper met with Winters to prepare for the opening of Windsor County Court's June term. "Mr. Darrow admits the case will be long and difficult, but he hopes to be able to assist in the defense," reported the *Vermont Journal*.[1]

State Detective E. A. Brown returned to Windsor amidst rumors "of newly discovered evidence favorable to the defense."[2] Brown was unable to substantiate them, but reports that Darrow was interviewing witnesses concerned Attorney General J. Ward Carver and Windsor County State's Attorney Lawrence Edgerton. They would be responsible for securing a murder conviction against a defendant represented by the nation's greatest defense lawyer.

On the afternoon of June 4, spectators again thronged the Woodstock courthouse anticipating the arrival of Clarence Darrow. Benches were filled and those who could not sit crowded the back of the courtroom. John Winters, "neatly dressed . . . sat unconcernedly between his wife and mother."[3] Herbert Tupper was at the defendant's table. Clarence Darrow was not.

Judge Frank Thompson opened the proceedings by requesting the defendant to stand before the court. "In the case of the *State v. John Winters*, in which the indictment charged the murder of Cecelia Gullivan, you pleaded not guilty. Do you now wish to change your former plea?" asked Thompson. "I do," answered Winters. "And how do you now plead?" said Thompson.[4]

"With his voice as calm as if he were passing the time of day," John Winters pleaded guilty to the murder of Cecelia Gullivan in the second degree.[5] Judge Thompson did not delay the sentencing. "I hereby impose the sentence provided by law and that is that you shall be confined at hard labor in the state's prison for the duration of your natural life," declared the judge.[6]

It took less than ten minutes for a "story filled with human drama and strange episodes" to end. There would be no retrial. To those who believed John Winters had been wrongly convicted, the admission of guilt "came as a sensation."[7]

The defendant, no stranger to shaping a story, held a remarkable colloquy with reporters after his plea. "I suppose everyone will think I really killed her now, won't they? But I didn't and God knows I didn't," said Winters with the earnestness that captivated friends and family, if not juries.

He maintained that his guilty plea was only for the sake of his family. "If I had been unmarried, I would have fought it . . . but it's different when a man is married. I had two children when they took me off to jail, I have three now. As I lay in my cell, those hundreds of nights trying to sleep, all I could think of was the horror those youngsters would have to face all their lives—knowing their father was put to death."[8]

The sincerity of his explanation could not be tested nor, then, could his denial that Clarence Darrow advised him to change his plea. "I figured out for myself that it would be the best way," Winters asserted.[9] But Darrow had put his advice in writing.

Darrow's papers contain a letter written to his Vermont co-counsel after the supreme court reversed the conviction of Winters for first-degree murder. The prosecution proposed a plea deal: a plea of guilty to second-degree murder for which the maximum penalty was life imprisonment, not death.

"There is no doubt in my mind that John should plead guilty," wrote Darrow. "There isn't a chance that the jury will acquit him. To stand against it means death. It is a serious responsibility for anyone to take. I would not think of taking it."[10]

The guilty plea was a sobering reminder to Vermonters that Cecelia Gullivan's death was "one of the most brutal in the annals of crime in this State."[11] A commentary in the *Barre Times*, widely reprinted in other newspapers, asserted that "there has been too much maudlin sentimentality about this crime . . . It is just as heinous three years after as at the moment it was committed."[12]

The public reassessment of the "cold fact" of the admission of guilt took refuge in the conventional wisdom that a life sentence in Vermont would mean just that. "Attorneys explained that a life sentence in most states meant imprisonment for 25 to 30 years but in Vermont, there is no time off for good behavior. The prisoner is confined as long as he lives."[13]

Clarence Darrow knew better. In his letter urging his Vermont co-counsel to persuade Winters to plead guilty, he wrote, "The case is now where John's life can be saved and sometime, he will get out."[14]

"Winters to be Pardoned" headlined the *Rutland Herald* on August 17, 1949. One week later the *New York Times* declared, "Slayer Saved by Darrow Paroled: A murderer who owes his life to the pleading of Clarence Darrow, twenty years ago walked out of State Prison today on parole. Winters was sentenced to die in the electric chair but was saved by the Chicago lawyer because of an old-time family debt."[15]

The prison file of John Winters does not, at first glance, appear to make him an appropriate candidate for a pardon with parole. "His history as given by those in charge would indicate he has an extremely unreasonable temperament and is ruled by impulse," said a report by an examining physician. A second report observed, "This man is inclined to blame others for his troubles. He thinks his lawyers betrayed him to begin with."[16]

But the key to the release of John Winters is found in his Vermont State Prison Dispensary and Hospital record. An entry on April 22, 1942, read "Diagnosis: Tuberculosis." Five years later, a note stated, "It is a problem how to handle him. Our facilities are not correct to handle active TB cases."[17]

The illness did not make him a model prisoner, but Winters knew something about "the modern treatment he thinks that is his due." He could get well, Winters told the facility doctor, "if he could be stripped to the waist in the sun without being under the restriction of prison . . . He has his mind set on freedom."[18]

Governor Ernest Gibson confirmed that the decision to pardon and parole John Winters was because the prisoner suffered from tuberculosis.[19] The fifty-five-year-old Winters said "he would go to New Mexico to live in a home for the aged," reported the *New York Times*.[20]

John Winters died on October 14, 1964, at age seventy. The death certificate reads: "residence: Cioli Monastery, Jimez Springs, New Mexico. Cause of death: prostate cancer (one year); active pulmonary tuberculosis (thirty years)."[21]

Clarence Darrow did not believe in justice. He believed in mercy.

EPILOGUE

W HEN JOHN WINTERS RETURNED to Windsor State Prison in June 1929 after pleading guilty to the second-degree murder of Cecelia Gullivan, his world got better. He was moved from the death cell to confinement within the prison's general population. The world outside was about to get worse.

On "Black Tuesday," October 29, 1929, stock prices collapsed in the single most catastrophic day in market history. Clarence and Paul Darrow had virtually all their money in the market. One month before the debacle, Darrow sent his son a cable from London: "I don't like the look of things. All stocks are far too high . . . if there are big drops you might get caught very badly." He cabled anxiously again a few days later: "I am hoping you hurried the sales."[1]

Paul did not. He borrowed on margin to buy more stock. The Darrow fortune evaporated.

Darrow's wife could not forgive her stepson for using her husband's "impossible to replace" life savings. "I am in a predicament right now," Darrow wrote to a friend, "not so much that I am but Paul is and you know I think more of him than myself."[2] To his son he wrote, "Anyhow don't worry about any of it."[3]

The financial devastation to the Darrows in the wake of the crash of October 1929 was almost instantaneous. But catastrophic economic consequences for the country took months to unfold. The routines of life went on. The Vermont Supreme Court opened its November term by handing down nine unanimous decisions. If unanimity was an indicator of Chief Justice John Watson's relationship with his colleagues, all was well again.

One month later there was a new chief justice. John Watson died on December 7, 1929. He was succeeded a week later by Justice George Powers who, like Watson, was to serve more than thirty years. Succession by seniority provided an orderly court but it did not guarantee collegiality.

The vacancy on the Supreme Court was filled the same day by Chief Trial Judge Frank Thompson. Justice Julius Willcox resigned two years later.

By 1931, even the most fervent believers in the resurrection of "Coolidge prosperity" had lost faith. "It appears to be a business depression," said a member of the Federal Reserve Board.[4] In Northampton, Massachusetts, where Grace and Calvin Coolidge were now living, the former president gave a friend money to prevent a run on a local bank.[5] On January 5, 1933, two months after Herbert Hoover lost the presidency and two months before the inauguration of President Franklin Roosevelt, sixty-year-old Calvin Coolidge died of a heart attack.

When Coolidge was put to rest in the Plymouth Cemetery family plot, Vermonters knew the difference between the appearance and reality of a depression. The consequences that were to reshape a nation profoundly altered Windsor, Vermont. The machine-tool industry was decimated when manufacturing production collapsed. NAMCO closed its Windsor Plant and abandoned the "Block" that housed employees.

For Frank Cone, the contrast between his success in the Roaring Twenties and the challenges of his life after the murder of Cecelia Gullivan must have, at times, seemed overwhelming. Yet he persevered through the flood of 1927 and the depths of the Great Depression. He kept Cone Automatic Machine Company afloat, even extending credit to the Russian government for machine-tool orders to keep his men employed. In 1936 Cone, "the unassuming mechanical and manufacturing genius who came from a Vermont hill farm," succumbed to a heart attack shortly after leaving the factory floor.[6]

Clarence Darrow confronted the stark decade that followed the Roaring Twenties. "The truth is before these terrible times, I had about $300,000 . . . Paul had about the same, but he owed a large amount. I have been giving him every cent I have."[7] Darrow grasped every opportunity he could to replenish the family's finances.

It was a remarkable display of fortitude for the lawyer who believed *State v. Winters* was his last case. Darrow was still the nation's most famous attorney and there were always defendants anxious to retain him. Although he pleaded without fee for the life of a mentally incompetent teenager facing the death penalty, Darrow agreed to represent prominent defendants "at variance with what I felt and had stood for" because he needed the money.[8]

Well into his seventies, Darrow continued to lecture, debate, defend, and write. His autobiography, *The Story of My Life* (edited by Max Perkins), was a bestseller. Of his decision to represent Loeb and Leopold in 1925, he wrote, "I knew of no good reason for refusing, but I was sixty-eight years old and weary . . . No client of mine had ever been put to death."[9]

At eighty, Darrow was beyond weary. "He talks considerably but says nothing we can understand," wrote Paul, who was caring for his father. "Once in a while I can catch a word or two. He has been this way for most of the last six months."[10] Darrow died on March 13, 1938. His ashes were scattered in Chicago's Jackson Park.[11] There was no pine box and Clarence Darrow never lost a client to the death penalty.

Margaret ("Maggie") Cooley Winters died in 1943 while her son was still in prison. Her death certificate lists the "informant" of her passing as her sister-in-law Laura, Mrs. Arthur Cooley. The cause of death is attributed to "general paralysis" to which is added a scribbled note, "*of the insane.*"

In 1949, the *New York Times* devoted nearly as much space to the death of seventy-two-year-old Raymond Trainor, "the special prosecutor in the 1927 trial of John Winters," as it had, ten years before, to the death of John Sargent, former attorney general of the United States. Trainor, "one of Vermont's leading trial attorneys," was remembered for prosecuting Winters for the first-degree murder of "Miss Cecelia Gullivan, a prominent Windsor woman." Clarence Darrow, "noted Chicago lawyer," won a new trial for the defendant, the *Times* added.[12]

Judge Harrie Chase retired from the US Court of Appeals in 1954. Of Judge Chase's quarter-century on the Second Circuit, a legal historian wrote, "It is difficult to conceive of a judicial career of comparable length and importance cloaked in a greater degree of anonymity."[13]

Harrie Chase's younger brother Paul was appointed to the Vermont Supreme Court in 1953. He resigned three years later after it was revealed that he spent months in California while ignoring the cases assigned to him by the chief justice.[14]

Paul Darrow died in 1956. Despite his father's unceasing labors during the Depression, the Darrow fortune was never recovered. (Darrow's wife Ruby had to give up their apartment upon her husband's death and sell his books and personal belongings.)[15] Paul was able to cobble together a business career after the Depression.

Clarence Darrow did leave a legacy. Irving Stone's bestseller *Clarence Darrow for the Defense*, published in 1941, was the first of an extraordinary succession of books, movies, and plays that have made "the attorney for the damned" an almost mythical figure. Darrow would not have liked the embellishment.

But he might have been pleased by a remembrance of his son that appeared in the local paper of Greeley, Colorado, where Paul Darrow raised his family. Paul was remembered for his tolerance and humility. Clarence Darrow was recalled as a kindly grandfather delighted to play with his granddaughters and visit his son. The Darrows were "tremendously interested in people as such," wrote a contemporary who admired both.[16]

Laura Cooley died in 1957 at age seventy-seven. She was buried in the Dartmouth College Cemetery with her husband who predeceased her, and their son, Harry Arthur Cooley, killed in an accident more than a half-century earlier.

Nearly three decades after John Winters walked out of Windsor State Prison, it was closed. The same idealism and optimism that prompted earlier Vermont legislatures and governors to seek to reform crime and punishment led to community-based correctional facilities. The last use of the electric chair was in 1954. Capital punishment in Vermont effectively ended in 1972.[17]

Windsor is no longer a prison town. The massive buildings of the prison were transformed by developers into "Olde Windsor Village," a complex of apartments surrounding a landscaped garden in the old prison yard. The stately houses that formed the Evarts compound are now residential care facilities for senior citizens.[18]

The NAMCO Block, built to house employees in the booming machine-tool industry of the Roaring Twenties, now provides low-income housing. The "birthplace of the precision tool industry" is remembered in Windsor's American Precision Museum. It is housed in the 1846 Robbins and Lawrence Armory and Machine Shop, a National Historic Landmark. The museum's "Machine Tool Hall of Fame" includes Frank Cone.[19]

Cecelia Gullivan is remembered differently. A restaurant is in the old railroad station near the spot where John Winters went looking for "a good time." The bar mixes creative cocktails, including "the Cecelia Gullivan": *Barr Hill Gin, Solerno Blood Orange Liqueur, grapefruit juice, basil simple syrup, Metcalfe's Raspberry Liqueur shaken into a martini. Murdered in the early hours of Nov 7, 1926, an executive at Windsor's Cone Automotive. Wounds to her face were so severe, they removed her head, preserved it in a jar and put it on display as evidence. Cecelia watched her own murder trial.*[20]

Liquor, murder, and celebrity. A touch of the Roaring Twenties—right here in Vermont.

NOTES

PROLOGUE: The Letter

1. John A. Farrell, *Clarence Darrow: Attorney for the Damned* (New York: Vintage Books Edition, 2011), 334.
2. Ibid., 12. "Attorney for the Damned" was the title of an article about Darrow by Lincoln Steffens in the *Saturday Review*, 27 February 1932.
3. Randall Tietjen, ed., *In the Clutches of the Law: Clarence Darrow's Letters* (Berkeley: University of California Press, 2013), 330–31.
4. "Darrow May Go to Winters Aid," *Boston Globe*, 3 June 1927.

CHAPTER 1: The Accident

1. Larry Coffin, "Working Horses in the Upper Valley Have a Rich and Varied History," Valley News, 14 October 2019. The author notes that "in the early 1900s horses were often frightened when they met automobiles on the road."
2. "Darrow May Go to Winters Aid," *Boston Globe*, 3 June 1927.
3. Ibid.
4. Ludlow *Vermont Tribune*, 12 November 1926.
5. Frederick Lewis Allen, *Only Yesterday: An Informal History of the 1920s* (New York: Harper & Row, 1931; New York: Harper Perennial Modern Classics, 2010), 186.
6. Ibid.

CHAPTER 2: Cecelia's Day

1. Guy Hubbard, "Leadership of Early Windsor Industries in the Mechanic Arts," *Proceedings of the Vermont Historical Society for the Years 1921, 1922, 1923* (Montpelier, VT: Capital City Press, 1924), 157–82.
2. American Precision Museum, https://americanprecision.org/category/about_page/.
3. Alan Earls, "Celebrating America's Love Affair with Machining," last modified 10 March 2022, https://todaysmachiningworld.com/magazine.
4. Guy Hubbard, *Frank Lyman Cone, Machine Tool Builder, 1868–1936: A Biographical Sketch* (Windsor, VT: privately printed, 1941), 18.

5. Jeremiah M. Evarts, *Recollections of a Vermonter, 1896–1918* (privately printed), New York, 12 Leahy Library, Vermont Historical Society.

6. "Frank Lyman Cone," Manufacturing Ledger, https//ledger.americanprecision.org.

7. *State v. Winters*, Woodstock Superior Court, 1926, trial transcript (3 volumes, 1–1,032), 3: 706, Vermont State Archives and Records Administration, Middlesex, hereafter cited as *Winters*.

8. Hubbard, *Cone*, 18.

9. Bret Waters, "The Women Who Built Silicon Valley," last modified 24 June 2020, https://thebolditalic.com. Waters noted that in its formative years "Silicon Valley was, without question, a male-dominated culture."

10. "Think Windsor Woman's Slayer is Ex-Convict," *Springfield* (VT) *Reporter*, 11 November 1926.

11. "Windsor Woman is Found Slain on Her Sleeping Porch," *Rutland* (VT) *Herald*, 9 November 1926.

12. Hubbard, *Cone*, 25.

13. *Winters*, 2: 534.

14. "Murderous Attacks on Two Women Stir Windsor to High Pitch," *Vermont Tribune*, 12 November 1926.

15. *Winters*, 3: 696.

16. *Winters*, 3: 708.

CHAPTER 3: **Winters' Night**

1. Frederick Lewis Allen, *Only Yesterday: An Informal History of the 1920s* (New York: Harper & Row, 1931; New York: Harper Perennial Modern Classics, 2010), 159.

2. "Minister Flays Authorities," *Boston Globe*, 16 November 1926.

3. Daniel Okrent, *Last Call: The Rise and Fall of Prohibition* (New York: Scribner, 2010), 234, 260.

4. "John Winters Charged with Robbery at Hanover, N.H.," *Barre* (VT) *Daily Times*, 21 October 1912.

5. *State v. Winters*, Woodstock Superior Court, 1926, trial transcript (3 volumes, 1–1,032), 2: 422, Vermont State Archives and Records Administration, Middlesex.

6. "Winters' Night of Aimless Intoxication," Windsor *Vermont Journal*, 19 November 1926 (from the *Rutland* [VT] *Herald*).

CHAPTER 4: **Paradise**

1. "Maxfield Parrish, a Mechanic Who Painted Fantastically," *New England Historical Society*, 30 March 2014, https://newenglandhistoricalsociety.com/maxfield-parrish-mechanic-painted-fantastically/.

2. "Mr. Evarts's Golden Wedding," *New York Times*, 27 August 1893.

3. Kevin O'Connor, "Famed Editor Maxwell Perkins Loved Windsor Best," West Lebanon, NH, *Valley News*, 10 June 2016.

4. A. Scott Berg, *Max Perkins: Editor of Genius* (New York: New American Library, paperback edition, 2016), 22.

5. *State v. Winters*, Woodstock Superior Court,1926, trial transcript (3 volumes, 1–1,032), 2: 639, Vermont State Archives and Records Administration, Middlesex.

6. "Windsor Woman is Found Slain on Her Sleeping Porch," *Rutland* (VT) *Herald*, 9 November 1926.

CHAPTER 5: **Murder!**

1. *State v. Winters*, Woodstock Superior Court,1926, trial transcript (3 volumes, 1–1,032), 3: 731, Vermont State Archives and Records Administration, Middlesex.

2. Ibid., 3: 700.

3. Ibid., 3: 701.

4. "Murderous Attacks on Two Women Stir Windsor to High Pitch," Ludlow *Vermont Tribune*, 12 November 1926.

5. "New Turn in Investigation of Woman Murder in Vermont," *Boston Globe*, 12 November 1926.

6. The *Brockton Daily Times* account of the services is quoted in "Hearing Set for Nov. 23," Windsor *Vermont Journal*, 19 November 1926; "Mrs Gullivan Faints on Seeing Daughter's Body," *Boston Globe*, 11 November 1926.

7. Henry F. Black, "Memorial to Raymond Trainor," *Hartford [VT] Historical Society Newslette*r, 26, 1 (September–October 2013): 6.

8. "Lapine Given Heavy Penalty," *Montpelier* (VT) *Morning Journal*, 9 January 1913.

9. Criminal investigations in Vermont were largely dependent on the competence of the county sheriff's office or police department if the crime occurred in one of the twelve municipalities that had one. The legislature resisted several attempts to create a statewide police agency until the failure of local authorities to find a trace of evidence when a Bennington College student disappeared on the Long Trail in 1946 led to the establishment of the Vermont State Police in 1947. http://www.terrymarin.us/VSPHistory.htmhttp://www.terrymartin.us/VSPHhistory.ht.

CHAPTER 6: **Prison Town**

1. Gene Smith, "In Windsor Prison," *American Heritage* 47, 3 (May/June 1996).

2. *Selectmen of Windsor v. Jacob*, 1 Tyl. 241 (1802).

3. Mark Bushnell, "Then Again: Trouble at State Prisons is Nothing New," *VTDigger*, 30 September 2018.

4. "The Vermont State Prison: Biennial Report of the Superintendent, 1916–1918," in *Biennial Report of the Director of State Institutions of the State of Vermont, for the term ending June 1918* (Rutland, VT: Tuttle Company, 1918), available online at https://cr.middlebury.edu/amlit_civ/

allen/VT_Institutions/desktop-vt-institutions-3-31-20/Biennial_Rept_Super-intendent_VSP_1918.pdf.

5. "Lapine Given Heavy Penalty," *Montpelier* (VT) *Morning Journal,* 9 January 1913.

6. "Did Not Escape from State's Prison," *St. Albans* (VT) *Messenger,* 10 April 1913.

7. "For the Public Safety" Windsor *Vermont Journal,* 19 November 1926.

8. NAMCO Block, https://en.m.wikipedia.org/wiki/NAMCO_Block.

9. "Winters to Face Attack Charge," *Boston Globe,* 13 November 1926.

CHAPTER 7: A Suspect

1. "Murderous Attacks on Two Women Stir Windsor to High Pitch," Ludlow *Vermont Tribune,* 12 November 1926.

2. "Winters Nervous as Inquest Begins in Windsor Murder," *Rutland* (VT) *Herald,* 11 November 1926.

3. *State v. Fairbanks,* 101 Vt 286, 290 (1929).

4. "Sheriff Fairbanks and Irma Stoodley Both Sentenced," *Rutland Herald,* 4 November 1926.

5. "Winters Nervous."

6. *State v. Winters,* Woodstock Superior Court, 1926, trial transcript (3 volumes, 1–1,032), 3: 908, Vermont State Archives and Records Administration, Middlesex, hereafter cited as *Winters.*

7. Ibid., 3: 909.

8. "Winters Nervous."

9. *Winters,* 2: 387.

10. *Winters,* 3: 911–12.

11. Ibid., 917.

12. "Winters Accused of Slaying Woman," Woodstock *Vermont Standard,* 18 November 1926.

13. "Winters Will be Arraigned Today as Windsor Slayer," *Rutland Herald,* 15 November 1926.

14. *Winters,* 3: 922. There was no constitutional obligation for the State to advise a defendant in custody of the right to an attorney (or the right to remain silent) until the US Supreme Court determined in 1966 that procedural safeguards (commonly known as "Miranda warnings") are required in a custodial interrogation. *Miranda v. Arizona,* 384 U.S. 436 (1966). The decision of Judge Frank Thompson to allow the statement obtained from Winters despite being the product of five days of questioning in a death cell was consistent with Vermont law in 1927. Only five years earlier, the Vermont Supreme Court held that a determination of whether a statement or confession was "voluntary" is to be made by the trial judge. The court cited as precedent a confession procured from a defendant who was chained to the floor in solitary confinement. *State v. Long,* 95 Vt. 485, 491 (1922).

CHAPTER 8: **Game On**

1. Randall Tietjen, ed., *In the Clutches of the Law: Clarence Darrow's Letters* (Berkeley: University of California Press, 2013), 374.
2. "Shift in Plan to Arraign Winters," *Boston Globe*, 17 November 1926.
3. "Deny Winters is Near Nervous Breakdown," *Rutland* (VT) *Herald*, 20 November 1926.
4. Ibid.
5. "Accused Man in Death Cell for More Than Two Weeks," *Boston Globe*, 24 November 1926.
6. Ibid.
7. Ibid.
8. "Nurse Says Winters Threatened to Kill Her," *Boston Globe*, 23 November 1926.
9. "Winters Case Will Await Grand Jury," *Rutland Herald*, 2 December 1926.
10. "John Winters Free of Murder," *Brattleboro* (VT) *Reformer*, 1 December 1926.
11. Vermont prosecutors are much more likely to use inquests than grand juries. Like the latter, witnesses are examined in secrecy before a judge. Defense attorneys are not present. But unlike a grand jury, a prosecutor cannot use an inquest to indict. A criminal charge can only be filed after a court finds probable cause based on the charging documents filed by the State. The office of attorney general never used a grand jury to indict a defendant in the twelve years (1985–1997) this author served as Vermont's attorney general.
12. "Winters Case Sensation of Legal Season," *Rutland* (VT) *News*, 18 December 1926.
13. "Winters May Go on Trial in Jan.," *Rutland News*, 9 December 1926.

CHAPTER 9: **The State's Case**

1. Connie Cain Ramsey, "The Side Judge: A History of Vermont's Assistant Judge," vt.assistantjudges.org/what-we-do/.
2. "To Exhibit Head of Miss Gullivan," *Boston Globe*, 22 January 1927.
3. D. Gregory Sanford, "From Ballot Box to Jury Box," Barre (VT) *Times-Argus*, 3 March 2008. Sanford notes that although eighteen states provided for women jurors in 1923, legislation introduced that year in Vermont was defeated. Judge Frank Thompson, then serving as a legislator, said the Vermont constitution might *prohibit* women jurors. A statewide referendum enabling women to serve on juries was approved by voters in November 1942.
4. *Norwich University Record*, 19, 16 (28 January 1928): 208.
5. *State v. Winters*, Woodstock Superior Court, 1926, trial transcript (3 volumes, 1–1,032), 1: 88–97, Vermont State Archives and Records Administra-

tion, Middlesex. All trial excerpts in this chapter are from this same set of pages. Note on usage:

a. The proper title for a trial judge in Vermont is "superior court judge." I have in this book referred to Judge Thompson and other superior court judges as "trial judges" because the difference between "superior" and "supreme" (the proper title for a justice on the supreme court) may be confusing to nonlawyers. (Lawyers seldom confuse the two. Judges never do.)

b. In the legalese of the 1920s, "respondent" was used instead of "defendant." Its use now would confuse lawyers and nonlawyers alike. I use defendant in the text even if, for example, John Winters is called the respondent.

c. In referring to Dr. Fred Kent and his autopsy testimony, I have used "medical examiner," a phrase that is in common usage and more accurately describes his role in *State v. Winters* than did his job title, "Assistant Director of the State Laboratory of Hygiene."

CHAPTER 10: **Exhibit 35**

1. "To Exhibit Head of Miss Gullivan," *Boston Globe*, 22 January 1927.
2. *State v. Winters*, Woodstock Superior Court, 1926, trial transcript (3 volumes, 1–1,032), Vermont State Archives and Records Administration, Middlesex. All trial excerpts in this chapter are from 1: 127–59, 2: 360–79.
3. *Boston Globe*, 22 January 1927.
4. A prosecutor's use of a plaster head as an exhibit was reversible error because "the nature of the demonstration and the distinctly feminine appearance of the clay head used by the medical examiner to explain the blow was certain to evoke an emotional response in the minds of the jurors." *Taylor v. State*, 640 So.2d 1127, 1134 (1994).
5. "Winters Trial at Woodstock," *Bethel* (VT) *Courier*, 27 January 1927.
6. First Degree Murder Convictions Vermont 1900–1985, Vermont Department of Corrections, Division of Planning and Research, 26 February 1986. Lib-861. Vermont State Archives and Records Administration, Middlesex.
7. "Murder Jury Sees Gruesome Exhibit," *Rutland* (VT) *Herald*, 27 January 1927.

CHAPTER 11: **The Link in the Chain**

1. *State v. Winters*, Woodstock Superior Court, 1926, trial transcript (3 volumes, 1–1,032), Vermont State Archives and Records Administration, Middlesex. All trial excerpts in this chapter are from 2: 424–39, 556–624, 3: 805–7.

CHAPTER 12: **The Defense**

1. *State v. Winters*, Woodstock Superior Court,1926, trial transcript (3 volumes, 1–1,032), Vermont State Archives and Records Administration,

Middlesex. All trial excerpts in this chapter are from 3: 858, 880–965, 970, 978–82.

2. *Rutland* (VT) *Herald*, 10 February 1927.

CHAPTER 13: **The Verdict**

1. "Arguments Begin in Winters Trial," *Boston Globe*, 17 February 1927.

2. *Rutland* (VT) *Herald*, 18 February 1927.

3. Ibid.

4. "Winters Guilty in First Degree," *Brattleboro* (VT) *Reformer*, February 19 1927.

5. "Winters Found Guilty in First Degree," St. Johnsbury, VT, *Caledonian Record*, February 19 1927.

6. "John C. Winters is Found Guilty in First Degree," *Burlington* (VT) *Daily News*, February 19 1927.

7. Ibid.

8. "Winters Found Guilty."

9. *State v. Winters*, Woodstock Superior Court, 1926, trial transcript (3 volumes, 1–1,032), 3: 1,031, Vermont State Archives and Records Administration, Middlesex.

CHAPTER 14: **Sons**

1. John A. Farrell, *Clarence Darrow: Attorney for the Damned* (New York: Vintage Books Edition, 2011), 90.

2. Ibid., 87.

3. Randall Tietjen, ed., *In the Clutches of the Law: Clarence Darrow's Letters* (Berkeley: University of California Press, 2013), 123, 126.

4. Ibid., 127.

5. Ibid., 126.

6. Ibid., 22.

7. Ibid.

8. Ibid., 339.

9. Clarence Darrow, *The Story of My Life* (New York: Charles Scribner's Sons, 1932; Boston: Da Capo Press, 1996), 32.

10. *Rutland* (VT) *Herald*, 13 August 1895; 22 March 1904; 17 May 1905; 2 February 1909.

11. Darrow, *Story*, 338.

12. Tietjen, *Letters*, 331.

13. Darrow, *Story*, 347.

CHAPTER 15: **Darrow and the Death Penalty**

1. Clarence Darrow, *The Story of My Life* (New York: Charles Scribner's Sons, 1932; Boston: Da Capo Press, 1996), 15.

2. Ibid., 361.

3. Arthur Weinberg, ed., *Attorney for the Damned: Clarence Darrow in the*

Courtroom (Chicago: University of Chicago Press 2012), 96.

4. Ibid., 103.

5. Ibid., 95.

6. Gene X. Smith, "In Windsor Prison," *American Heritage* 47, 3, american-heritage.com/mayjune-1996.

7. Randolph Roth, "'Blood Calls for Vengeance!' The History of Capital Punishment in Vermont," *Proceedings of the Vermont Historical Society* 65, 1 & 2 (Winter/Spring 1997), 17.

8. Ibid., 17–18.

9. Smith, "In Windsor Prison."

10. Roth, "'Blood Calls for Vengeance!'" 18.

11. Ibid., 17.

12. "Report of the Select Committee on House Bill No. 146 Entitled 'An Act to Abolish the Punishment of Death,'" in *Journal of the House of Representatives of the State of Vermont, October Session, 1859* (Montpelier, VT: E. P. Walton, 1859), 406.

13. Darrow, *Story*, 219–20.

14. John Stark Bellamy II, *Vintage Vermont Villainies: True Tales of Murder & Mystery from the 19th and 20th Centuries* (Woodstock, VT: Countryman Press, 2007), 60.

15. Smith, "In Windsor Prison."

16. Bellamy, *Vintage Vermont Villainies*, 54.

17. Ibid., 56.

18. Justice John Watson, then a junior member of the Vermont Supreme Court, wrote the opinion rejecting the claim that the defendant had limited mental capacity. "She coolly and deliberately engaged in a business transaction . . . to effect the death of her husband . . . get his life insurance and marry [another]." *Rogers v. State*, 77 Vt. 454, 485 (1905).

19. Bellamy, *Vintage Vermont Villainies*, 59.

20. Ibid., 63

21. "The Kent Hanging," *Rutland* (VT) *Herald*, 8 January 1912.

22. Mariessa Dobrick, "History Space: First Use of VT Electric Chair," *Burlington* (VT) *Free Press*, 17 March 2018; death penaltyinfo.org/state-and-federal-info/state-by-state/newyork.

23. John A. Farrell, *Clarence Darrow: Attorney for the Damned* (New York: Vintage Books Edition, 2011), 479.

24. Ibid., 50–1.

25. *Acts and Resolves Passed by the General Assembly of the State of Vermont at the Twenty-Second Biennial Session, 1912* (Montpelier, VT: Capital City Press, 1913), Public Acts, sec. 2372.

26. "George Warner Dies in Electric Chair in First Execution to Take Place in State, Superseding Hangman's Rope," *St. Albans* (VT) *Messenger*, 17 July 1919.

27. deathpenaltyusa.org/usa1/date/1920.htm.
28. Darrow, *Story*, 232.
29. Weinberg, *Attorney for the Damned*, 23.
30. Ibid., 19
31. Ibid., 47
32. Ibid., 50, 53.
33. Ibid., 51–2.
34. Farrell, *Clarence Darrow*, 360.
35. "Darrow Plans to Retire," *New York Times*, 14 April 1927.

CHAPTER 16: Exceptions

1. Amity Shlaes, *Coolidge* (New York: HarperCollins, 2013), 365. A. Scott Berg, *Lindbergh* (New York: Berkeley Books,1999), 154.
2. Frederick Lewis Allen, *Only Yesterday: An Informal History of the 1920s* (New York: Harper & Row, 1931; New York: Harper Perennial Modern Classics, 2010), 190–91.
3. *Boston Globe*, 3 June 1927.
4. Brief for Respondent, *State v. Winters*, No. 1227 A, Vermont Supreme Court, January Term, 1928, 1. http://moses.law.umn.edu/darrow/documents/State_of_Vermont_v_Winters_brief.pdf
5. "Refusal of the Lower Court to Admit Testimony Concerning Blood Should Give Prisoner Winters a New Trial," *Montpelier* (VT) *Evening Argus*, 13 January 1928.
6. Brief, 7.
7. Ibid., 21.
8. Ibid., 22.

CHAPTER 17: Darrow Arrives

1. "Winters Case Draws Crowd," *Barre* (VT) *Daily Times*, 12 January 1928.
2. "Justice Harrie Chase on the 'Ambassador,'" *Burlington* (VT) *Free Press*, 8 November 1927.
3. Amity Shlaes, *Coolidge* (New York: HarperCollins, 2013), 400–1. In 1928 Congress appropriated and Vermont received $2,654,000 for road and bridge repair. See Michael Sherman, Gene Sessions, and P. Jeffrey Potash, *Freedom and Unity: A History of Vermont* (Barre: Vermont Historical Society, 2004), 426–27.
4. Randall Tietjen, ed., *In the Clutches of the Law: Clarence Darrow's Letters* (Berkeley: University of California Press, 2013), 288; Caroline Taggart, *All That Glisters . . . and Other Quotations You Should Know* (London: Michael O'Mara Books Limited, 2018).
5. "One Man's Life as Important as Another, States Clarence Darrow Who is Defending John Winters," *Montpelier* (VT) *Evening Argus*, 10 January 1928.
6. "Clarence Darrow," *Brattleboro* (VT) *Reformer*, 10 January 1928.

7. "Editorial," St. Johnsbury, VT, *Caledonian Record*, 12 January 1928.

8. "Press Comment," *Middlebury* (VT) *Register*, 13 January 1928.

9. "Darrow Will Plead Case of John Winters," *Caledonian Record*, 10 January 1928.

10. "Supreme Court in New Hall of Justice," *Burlington Free Press*, 9 May 1918.

11. Paul S. Gillies, *The Law of the Hills: A Judicial History of Vermont* (Barre: Vermont Historical Society, 2019), 46, 143.

12. *State v Tubbs*, 101 Vt. 5 (1928).

13. "Windsor County Court," Windsor *Vermont Journal*, 8 July 1927.

14. "Darrow to Argue in Behalf of Winters," *Montpelier Evening Argus*, 12 January 1928.

15. Ibid.

16. "Darrow Gives Plea to Fulfil Pledge," *New York Times*, 13 January 1928.

17. "Darrow Redeems Old-Time Pledge," *Vermont Journal*, 13 January 1928.

18. "Winters Case Draws Crowd," *Barre Daily Times*, 12 January 1928.

19. "Darrow Redeems Old-Time Pledge."

20. "Darrow Pleads for John Winters Today," *Springfield* (VT) *Reporter*, 12 January 1928.

21. "Darrow Redeems Old-Time Pledge."

22. Ibid.

23. "Darrow Draws Crowd to Court," *Brattleboro Reformer*, 13 January 1928.

24. Ibid.

25. Ibid.

26. Ibid.

27. "Clarence Darrow Pleads for Winters," *Burlington Free Press*, 13 January 1928.

28. "Darrow Draws Crowd."

29. "Darrow Gives Plea."

30. "Clarence Darrow Pleads."

31. "Darrow Draws Crowd."

32. "Darrow Gives Plea."

33. "Darrow Draws Crowd."

CHAPTER 18: Deadlock

1. Amity Shlaes, *Coolidge* (New York: HarperCollins, 2013), 381.

2. Frederick Lewis Allen, *Only Yesterday: An Informal History of the 1920s* (New York: Harper & Row, 1931; New York: Harper Perennial Modern Classics, 2010), 254.

3. *State v. Fairbanks*, 101 Vt. 30, 35 (1928).

4. Ibid.

5. John A. Farrell, *Clarence Darrow: Attorney for the Damned* (New York: Vintage Books Edition, 2011), 436.

6. Paul S. Gillies, *The Law of the Hills: A Judicial History of Vermont* (Barre: Vermont Historical Society, 2019), 309.

7. "An Address Delivered by Chief Justice Watson Before the Vermont Bar Association, January 4,1921," 94 Vt. 501–25 (1921). Watson was prompted by what he considered to be inaccurate comments about the constitutional prohibition of slavery in Vermont. His essay exhibited his heartfelt passion for his native state ("We love Vermont. We are proud of her history."), but of greater significance is his assertion that the Vermont Constitution's prohibition of slavery is "self-executing . . . complete in itself and needs no legislative action to put it in force." Watson considered any other interpretation "repugnant to the spirit of the instrument." The chief justice's profound belief that "the spirit of the Constitution, collected from its words, is to be respected not less than the letter" is a worthy guide for his successors. Ibid., 501, 516, 524. For a fuller appreciation of Chief Justice Watson, see Paul S. Gillies, "A Hero Once, A Judge for Life," *Vermont Bar Journal* 37 (Winter 2012): 7–16.

8. *State v. Romano*, 101 Vt. 53 (1928).

9. Cases heard by supreme courts in states without intermediate appellate courts are of far greater variety than cases heard by the US Supreme Court and states that have such courts. In Vermont litigants can appeal directly to the supreme court from the trial court. Other rural states are similar. When the author was appointed to the Vermont Supreme Court, he received a note from Justice David Souter, who had served on the New Hampshire Supreme Court. It read, "Welcome to the general practice of the law." He would not have been surprised by a banana case.

10. *State v. Lapan*, 101 Vt. 124, 130 (1928).

11. *State v. Zielonko*, 101 Vt. 105, 107 (1928).

12. *State v. Lapan.*

13. "Biennial Report of the Attorney General for the Two Years ending June 30, 1928," 4, in *Vermont Public Documents, Being Reports of State Officers, Departments, and Institutions for the Two Years Ending June 30, 1928* (Rutland, VT: Tuttle Company, 1928).

14. *Leonard v Willcox, et al.*, 101 Vt. 195, 215 (1928).

15. Ibid., 217.

16. Ibid., 219.

CHAPTER 19: Wunderkind

1. Amity Shlaes, *Coolidge* (New York: HarperCollins, 2013), 428–29.

2. Ibid., 329.

3. Ibid.

4. "National Affairs," *Time* magazine, 30 March 1925.

5. Shlaes, *Coolidge*, 401.

6. "Fairbanks Found Guilty Gets Two Years in Jail," *Rutland* (VT) *Herald*, 8 November 1928. The Vermont Supreme Court again reversed the sheriff's conviction for adultery. The reversal is difficult to explain if one relies solely on the legal analysis in Justice Julius Willcox's opinion. *State v. Fairbanks*, 102 Vt. 283 (1929).

7. *Saliba v. New York Central R.R. Co.*, 101 Vt. 427, 431 (1928).

8. Shlaes, *Coolidge*, 434.

9. "Honor for Vermont," *Barre* (VT) *Daily Times*, 28 January 1929.

10. Ibid.

11. "United States Court of Appeals for the Second Circuit," Wikipedia, last edited 20 May 2024.

12. Earle S. Kinsley, *Recollections of Vermonters in State and National Affairs* (Rutland, VT: privately printed, 1946), 119–20.

13. Ibid., 134.

14. Ibid., 135.

15. Marin Schick, *Learned Hand's Court* (Baltimore: Johns Hopkins University Press, 2019), 33.

16. See Note, *Town of Duxbury v. Town of Williamstown*, 102 Vt. 94, 98 (1929). "When this case was heard it was assigned to Justice Chase. Upon his retirement from the Bench and at the February term, it was reassigned." *Trustees of Newport Center v. Niles*, et. al. 102 Vt. 121, 124 (1929) (same).

17. *Burlington* (VT) *Free Press*, 21 January 1929.

18. Ibid.

19. When the author was nominated to be chief justice of the Vermont Supreme Court, he was urged to resign his position as attorney general in advance of confirmation upon assurance that he would be easily confirmed. Like Chase, he demurred.

20. "Two Different Courts," *St. Albans* (VT) *Messenger*, 4 February 1929.

21. "Senate Confirms Nomination of Judge Chase to Circuit Court," *Brattleboro* (VT) *Reformer*, 1 February 1929.

CHAPTER 20: "The Peculiar Circumstances"

1. Paul S. Gillies, *The Law of the Hills: A Judicial History of Vermont* (Barre: Vermont Historical Society, 2019), 138–39. Gillies notes that "with very few exceptions, the legislature had for many years elected the same Court year after year, replacing those who died, or retired, and moving each remaining judge up the rank." When a governor "meddled . . . with the grand principle of seniority" it precipitated a judicial and constitutional crisis that was resolved only when the order of seniority was reestablished by the legislature. Ibid. 138–41.

2. "Reported Willcox Will Be Promoted," *Burlington* (VT) *Free Press*, 7 February 1929.

3. "No Reason for Delay," *St. Albans* (VT) *Messenger*, 4 February 1929.

4. "Reported Willcox Will Be Promoted."

5. "Willcox and Bicknell are Elected to Fill Two Court Vacancies," *Rutland* (VT) *Herald*, 8 February 1929.

6. "Clarence Darrow Here Yesterday in Conference Over Winters Case," Windsor *Vermont Journal*, 19 April 1929.

7. *Brattleboro* (VT) *Reformer*, 2 March 1929.

8. "Clarence Darrow Pleads for John C. Winters," Ludlow *Vermont Tribune*, 15 March 1929.

9. "Darrow Keeps Pledge by Saving Man's Life," *New York Times*, 13 January 1928.

10. "Clarence Darrow Pleads," *Vermont Tribune*, 15 March 1929.

11. "Appeals for New Trial for Winters," *Burlington Free Press*, 9 March 1929.

12. Kevin Boyle, *Arc of Justice: A Saga of Race, Civil Rights, and Murder in the Jazz Age* (New York: Picador, 2004), 234.

13. "Appeals for New Trial for Winters."

14. "Clarence Darrow Asks Supreme Court for New Trial for J. C. Winters," *Brattleboro Reformer*, 8 March 1929.

15. "Darrow Enjoys Trip Through Vermont," *St. Albans Messenger*, 11 March 1929.

16. Ibid.

17. *New York Times*, 13 March 1929.

18. "Peregrinations," *Rutland Herald*, 15 March 1929.

19. *State v. Winters*, 102 Vt. 36, 63 (1929).

20. Ibid.

21. Ibid., 65.

CHAPTER 21: **Winters' Time**

1. "Clarence Darrow Here Yesterday in Conference Over Winters Case," Windsor *Vermont Journal*, 19 April 1929.

2. "Darrow Conferred," *Montpelier* (VT) *Evening Argus*, 27 April 1929.

3. "Winters Gets Life Sentence," *Brattleboro* (VT) *Reformer*, 5 June 1929.

4. "Winters Makes 2nd Degree Murder Plea and Gets Life Term," *Rutland* (VT) *Herald*, 5 June 1929.

5. An intentional killing is murder in either the first or second degree. First-degree murder is premeditated. Second-degree murder is intentional but without premeditation or planning.

6. "Winters Makes 2nd Degree Murder Plea."

7. Ibid.

8. Ibid.

9. Ibid.

10. Randall Tietjen, ed., *In the Clutches of the Law: Clarence Darrow's Letters* (Berkeley: University of California Press, 2013), 373.

11. "John C. Winters Sentenced to Life Term," *Burlington* (VT) *Free Press*, 5 June 1929.

12. "The Winters Case, (Barre Times)" *St. Albans* (VT) *Messenger*, 7 June 1929.

13. "Winters Makes 2nd Degree Murder Plea."

14. Tietjen, ed., *In the Clutches of the Law*, 373.

15. *Rutland Herald,* 17 August 1949; *New York Times,* 25 August 1949.

16. Prison Record of John C. Winters, Physician's Reports of March 25, 1943, May 26, 1943. Vermont State Archives and Records Administration (VSARA), Middlesex.

17. Ibid., Vermont State Prison Dispensary and Hospital Record.

18. Ibid., May 6, 1947.

19. "Winters to Be Pardoned," *Rutland Herald,* 18 August 1949.

20. *New York Times,* 25 August 1949.

21. Certificate of Death, State of New Mexico. No.04167. Winters' death certificate reports his date of birth as June 27, 1896. His date of birth on his prison record is June 27, 1894. I am grateful to Mariessa Dobrick, VSARA, for her assistance in retrieving these records.

EPILOGUE

1. Randall Tietjen, ed., *In the Clutches of the Law: Clarence Darrow's Letters* (Berkeley: University of California Press, 2013), 382.

2. John A. Farrell, *Clarence Darrow: Attorney for the Damned* (New York: Vintage Books Edition, 2011), 439.

3. Tietjen, ed., *In the Clutches of the Law,* 383–84.

4. Frederick Lewis Allen, *Only Yesterday: An Informal History of the 1920s* (New York: Harper & Row, 1931; Harper Perennial Modern Classics, 2010), 297.

5. Amity Shlaes, *Coolidge* (New York: HarperCollins, 2013), 444.

6. Guy Hubbard, *Frank Lyman Cone, Machine Tool Builder, 1868–1936: A Biographical Sketch* (Windsor, VT: privately printed, 1941), 29.

7. Farrell, *Clarence Darrow,* 442–43.

8. Ibid., 447.

9. Clarence Darrow, *The Story of My Life* (New York: Charles Scribner's Sons, 1932; Da Capo Press, 1996), 232.

10. Farrell, *Clarence Darrow,* 465.

11. Ibid., 466.

12. "Raymond J. Trainor, Vermont Attorney," *New York Times,* 17 October 1949.

13. Martin Schick, *Learned Hand's Court* (Baltimore: Johns Hopkins University Press, 2019), 33. It was Harrie Chase's reputational misfortune to be on a court composed of some of the most brilliant judges in American legal history. The conventional perception of Judge Chase has been shaped by Gerald Gunther's biography of the incomparable Learned Hand, who wrote that Chase "preferred his outings on the golf course to his struggles with arguments and judicial opinions," *Learned Hand: The Man and the Judge,* 2d edition (Oxford: Oxford University Press, 2010), 244. Harrie B. Chase, https://en.wikipedia.org/wiki/Harrie_B._Chase, last edited 3 April 2024. Schick's view of Chase is more generous: "A first-rate craftsman and much underrated judge," 34.

14. "No Action Taken on Judge," *Burlington* (VT) *Daily News*, 8 April 1956; "Colleagues Request Chase's Resignation," *Burlington* (VT) *Free Press*, 7 July 1956.

15. Farrell, *Clarence Darrow*, 466.

16. "A Genial, Tolerant, Humble Man is Dead," *Greeley* (CO) *Tribune*, 21 December 1956. I am grateful to Randal Tietjen for providing this article.

17. The United States Supreme Court in *Furman v. Georgia*, 408 U.S. 238 (1972) compelled states that chose to retain capital punishment to amend their death penalty laws because of the arbitrariness of its imposition. States like Vermont that chose not to do so effectively eliminated capital punishment. The only Vermont crime that still carried a death penalty (treason) was amended in 2024 to a penalty of twenty-five years to life. In 2024 the legislature also repealed statutes relating to the imposition of the death penalty, including place of execution and number of witnesses. It is still possible for the death penalty to be imposed under federal law for murder, espionage, or treason if the defendant is convicted in federal court in Vermont.

18. Gene X. Smith, "In Windsor Prison," *American Heritage* 47, 3, american-heritage.com/mayjune-1996. Historic Homes of Runnemede, https:www.hhrliving.org.

19. NAMCO Block, https://en.wikipedia.org/wiki/NAMCO_Block, last edited 23 January 2022; American Precision Museum, americanprecision.org; Frank Lyman Cone, ledger.americanprecision.org.

20. The Windsor Station Restaurant, Specialty Cocktails, windsorstationvt.com.